CW01622225

Rich i[illegible]y:
Life in Hungate 1900-1938

Van Wilson
with photographs by
Simon I Hill FRPS

Published by the
Archaeological Resource Centre
St Saviourgate, York

with the support of

The Scirebröc Group
and
York Oral History Project

1996

Published by the Archaeological Resource Centre
St Saviourgate, York

3 February 1996

Copyright © Text - Van Wilson and interviewees 1996
Copyright © Photographs - Simon I Hill 1996

All rights reserved.

Van Wilson hereby asserts and gives notice of her right under Section 77 of the **Copyright, Designs and Patents Act 1988** to be identified as the author of this work.

Simon I Hill hereby asserts and gives notice of his right under Section 77 of the **Copyright, Designs and Patents Act 1988** to be identified as the author of all photographs dated '1995' appearing in this work.

British Library Cataloguing in Publication Data
The Catalogue Record for this book is available from the British Library

ISBN No. 1 874454 07 8

Design and layout is by The Scirebröc Group, York. Tel 01 904 672 350
Printing is by Quacks, York. Tel 01 904 635 967

Cover photograph
Flooding at Wray's Yard, Hungate, 28 February 1933.

Mrs Dorothy Reynolds, wife of Dr Reynolds,
with their two sons, circa.1930

Mrs Dorothy Reynolds, 1995

Contents

Introduction
by Hugh Bayley MP — *facing* 1

Preface — 1

Acknowledgements — 1

Profile of St Saviour's Residents — 2

1. The Environment — 7
- **The Parish** — 7
- **The Streets** — 12

2. A Child's Eye-View — 31
- **Pound Garth** — 39

3. Schooldays — 49
- **Haughton School** — 49
- **Bedern School** — 52
- **Castlegate School** — 54
- **Blue Coat School** — 58

4. Industry and the Workplace — 62
- **Leetham's Mill** — 63
- **The Gas Works** — 66
- **Slaughterhouses** — 72
- **Laundries** — 76

5. **A Wealth of Shops** 82
Pawnbrokers 95

6. **Leisure Time** 96
Linnet Singing 96
Sport 99
The Flying Flea 101
Cinema 102
Theatre 111

7. **Poverty and the Community Spirit** 116
Health and the Medical Profession 116
Poverty and the Community Spirit 126

About the author ... 140
About the photographer ... 140
About the ARC ... 141

Bibliography 142

List of Illustrations

Flooding at Wray's Yard, Hungate, 28 February 1933	*Cover*
Mrs Dorothy Reynolds, wife of Dr Reynolds, with their two sons, circa.1930	*opposite bibliographic information*
Mrs Dorothy Reynolds, 1995	
Floods in Lower Wesley Place, 1933	13
Garden Place, 1930s	14
Mrs Alice Butterworth, 1995	15
Alice Butterworth and her husband, Garden Street, 1923	16
Hungate Wide Yard, 1930s	18
Mrs Nellie Fearn, 1995	22
Nellie Goodwin, Dundas Street, 1934	23
George Squire, with his grandfather's watch, 1995	24
George Squire and his grandfather, Have Lane, 1927	25
Jack Birch, 1995	28
Stonebow House, 1995	30
Dundas Street, 1930s	32
The site of Pound Garth, 1995	39
Mrs Lavinia Kay, with old flat iron, 1995	45
Lavinia Lawson with mother and sister, Haymarket, 1932	46
Haughton School advertisement, York City Yearbook, 1921	50
Mrs Dorothy Cook, 1995	54
Dorothy Barker, Castlegate School, 1930	55
Ernest Webster, 1995	60
10, 11, 12 Drummond Street and WCs at rear of 31 Hungate, 1930s	61
Bellerby's Saw Mills, now Derwent Coachworks, 1995	62
Leetham's Mill, 1995	65
Mrs Chittock at a street party, Hungate, 1929	69
Louisa Grant, at a Women's Land Army Reunion, 1949	70

Mrs Louisa Aldrich, 1995 71
Yorkshire Laundries Ltd, Peasholme Green,
York City Yearbook, 1920 77
Fred Wright, Haulage Contractor,
Haymarket, 1930 79
Alf Huckle's Shop and Haymarket Inn, 1930s 84
Irene and Cecelia Thorpe, Stonebow Lane, 1934 86
Mrs Irene Thompson, 1995 87 *top*
Mrs Cecelia Felton, 1995 87
Valerie Shirbon, aged 10 89
Mrs Valerie Law, 1995 90
Waudby's fish shop, now an Italian restaurant,
Fossgate, 1995 92
The German Eagle, Fossgate, dated 1898 93
Harry Burnett and mother, 1920 94
Wheatsheaf Inn and Forage Warehouse, 1920s 97
Woolpack Inn and St Saviour's Place, 1930s 99
Woolpack Inn, now Minet Insurance,
and Blue Coat School, 1995 100
The Electric Theatre, now Macdonalds,
Fossgate, 1995 104
Mr and Mrs Hall, 1995 107
Mrs Rene Sheard, 1995 108
Mrs May Greenley, 1995 112
May Fearn, 1928 113
Rear of 1-17 Lower Wesley Place, 1930s 115
Samuel Thompson during World War II 119
Samuel Thompson, 1995 120
Dr Reynolds' election pamphlet, 1929 125
Andy Waudby in the army, 1939 131
Andy waudby with wooden toy marble rack, 1995 132
Wally Holmes, 1995 134
Wally Holmes as a young man 135
Hungate area, 1930 *Crown Copyright* 138
Hungate area, 1961 *Crown Copyright* 139

HUGH BAYLEY M.P.

HOUSE OF COMMONS
LONDON SW1A 0AA

This book is a vivid recollection of life in Hungate in the early years of this century. The story is told by men and women who lived there - some in appalling conditions of squalor - yet somehow they managed to maintain pride in themselves, their homes and their community.

They lived through a time of radical change. In his 1901 social survey of York, Seebohm Rowntree described Hungate as "one of the main slum districts in York." Fewer than half the houses had their own cold water tap. Forty years later the slums had been cleared and their inhabitants had moved to new council houses. One resident recalls the magic of moving into a council house with electric light.

It is a story told by survivors. The narrators are now well into retirement and some, sadly, have passed away before publication. At the turn of the century, one child in four living in Hungate died before their first birthday. By 1936 it was one child in 13. Now, with a National Health Service, it is one in 120 in North Yorkshire.

Despite the ugly Stonebow centre, which contaminates the heart of modern Hungate, York generally has been good at conserving its archaeology and historic buildings. This book, too, is a miracle of conservation - preserving ordinary citizens' memories of the past for future generations. It shows that history is too important to leave to historians. May it be a lasting tribute to the narrators who have shared their childhood with us.

Hugh Bayley

Hugh Bayley MP

Preface

The idea for this book came several years ago when York's Archaeological Resource Centre and the York Oral History Project decided to collaborate on an exploration of the recent history of St Saviour's parish.

In December 1991, the ARC invited, through the Press, residents and ex-residents of the parish, to come to an 'Open Day' where they were able to look around the old church of St Saviour's, where the ARC is based, and rekindle their memories of the area. Interested people were then interviewed in their own homes by various ARC and Oral History Project volunteers.

From that beginning, the interviews were transcribed, and edited extracts of these appear in the following pages, together with the results of background research which will set the scene. Although I have retained original names where possible, one or two have been omitted in order to avoid any unnecessary distress.

Van Wilson
York, 3 February 1996

Acknowledgements

Grateful thanks goes to several individuals and organisations who have generously contributed to the funding of this publication, namely: Mr Jack Birch, R M Burton Charitable Trust, Friends Central Adult School Trust, The Scirebröc Group, Sheldon Memorial Trust, Ms Julie Thompson, York Common Good Trust.

The 1930s photographs are used by kind permission of the York City Archives; the advertisements by kind permission of North Yorkshire County Council, and the maps by kind permission of the Ordnance Survey, with the consent of the Controller of Her Majesty's Stationery Office, Crown Copyright reserved.

All the work on this book has been done in a voluntary capacity, and I would like to thank Mr Hugh Bayley, Member of Parliament for York, for his introduction, the York Oral History Project committee (Joe Boutflower, Alan Hardwick, Philip Johnson and Mike Race), and the following interviewers: Janet Cowper, Michael Edison, and Karen Kadow, also Colin Thompson who spent several months on the project. I would also like to thank several members of staff at York Archaeological Trust, namely, Francis Mee, for reading the manuscript and making useful suggestions, Richard Briggs, for his computer advice in the initial stages of the project, and Simon Chew for production of the photographic screens prior to printing.

I am particularly indebted to Dr Andrew Jones, Director of the ARC, who conceived the original idea and set up the project, for his enthusiasm, guidance and encouragement throughout this work; and also to Simon I Hill, formerly Head of Photography at York Archaeological Trust, for taking the splendid portraits of many of the residents interviewed, the views of the Hungate area as it appears today, and for producing copies of many treasured and fragile photographs.

The biggest debt is, of course, to the residents themselves, who have supplied information about St Saviour's parish, and have allowed me to quote freely from their interviews. I feel very privileged to have met them and to have shared their stories.

Profile of St Saviour's Residents

Mrs Louisa Aldrich
Born Louisa Grant in 1919 in Webster's Passage off St Saviourgate, Mrs Aldrich now lives in Huntington. She attended Castlegate School and remembers a great deal about domestic life in the Hungate area. She went into service after school, then to work at Armstrong Oilers on Lendal Bridge, and later worked for Woodcocks bakers, doing much of the baking. During the Second World War, she was in the Women's Land Army.

Mr Jack Birch
Born in 1911 in St Saviourgate, Mr Birch is familiar with the architecture and buildings of the district. He attended Fishergate School and then joined his father's building firm. Today he is Managing Director of William Birch & Sons.

Mr Harry Burnett
Mr Burnett was born in 1920 and, until his death in early 1995, lived in Clifton with his wife Joyce, who came originally from Haver Lane. He attended Park Grove School and went to Centenary Chapel.

Mrs A Butterworth
Born Alice Harris in 1906, Mrs Butterworth lived in Garden Street but is now a Clifton resident. She was a pupil of Castlegate School, and also regularly went to the Band of Hope and the Hungate Mission Sunday School. She remembers playing on Pound Garth and talks about local characters and about Leetham's Mill, where her father worked.

Mr James Cave
Mr Cave was born in 1910 in St Saviourgate, and attended the nearby Haughton School. His memory covers many subjects, and he was able to provide a wealth of detail about people and places. Unfortunately, Mr Cave died in early 1995.

Mr Edward (Ted) Chittock
Mr Chittock, who now lives in Huntington, was born in Hungate and was a member of the York Boys' Club, which trained quite a few boxers, some of whom became well known. Mr Chittock remembers local characters, pubs and housing conditions. He stresses the strong community spirit which existed in the area.

Mrs Dorothy Cook
Mrs Cook was born in 1920 and lived in Hungate between the ages of 5 and 13. She went to Castlegate School and now lives in Wigginton. She is the granddaughter of Mr and Mrs Barker, the Hungate undertaker and midwife.

Mr Reg Deighton
Mr Deighton was born in 1925 and spent most of his childhood in St Andrewgate. He now lives in Acomb. He attended Bedern School, and helped out at Clancy's rag and bone dealers. He remembers the chicory works on Layerthorpe and the local competitions for linnet singing.

Mrs G Fearn
Born Nellie Goodwin in 1918, the daughter of a tailor, Mrs Fearn lived in Dundas Street until the age of 17 and now has her home in Clifton. She described the area as 'tough' yet at the same time, a warm and caring community.

Mrs J Felton and Mrs I Thompson
Mrs Thompson was born Irene Thorpe in 1926, and her sister Cecelia (Mrs Felton) in 1928, in Stonebow Lane. Their grandmother had a smallholding in Spen Lane, keeping goats and chickens, and their uncle raced whippets on Pound Garth. Their father, who served with the West Yorkshire Regiment in World War I, played the piano in the Woolpack. They both now live in Clifton.

Mrs Greenley
Born May Fearn in 1909, Mrs Greenley now lives in the Hull Road area. She spent many years in Spen Lane and remembers being poor but happy. Her family attended St Saviour's Church, and her mother took in theatrical lodgers. May herself danced in the chorus at the Empire but was not allowed to continue there, and had to go to work at Terry's.

Mr and Mrs J Hall

Mr Joseph (Stan) Hall was born in Broom's Court, Hungate, in 1911 and Mrs Lily Hall in Sawmill Lane, Hungate, in 1912. They married in 1935 and now live in the Groves. They talk about children's games, about friends, work, and life in the 1920s and 30s.

Mr Walter Holmes

Wally Holmes was born in 1925 in Dundas Street, and is now in Clifton. He remembers the popular Woolpack rugby team, and the many local tradesmen, bringing their goods by horse and cart. He talks about the Gas Company, the Electric Cinema and the pawnbrokers.

Mrs Lavinia Kay

Born Lavinia Lawson in St John's Place, Hungate, in 1925, Mrs Kay today lives in Acomb. She went to Bedern School, and played on Pound Garth. She remembers the appalling conditions in which families had to live, and colourful characters of the time.

Mrs Valerie Law

Valerie Shirbon lived at the sweet shop on the corner of St Saviourgate from the 1940s to 1960s but is now in Fulford. She helped in her mother's shop and met many of the local residents.

Mrs Dorothy Reynolds and Mr Guy King-Reynolds

Mrs Reynolds, who was born Dorothy Baker in 1903, was the wife of Dr Reynolds of St Saviourgate, and Mr King-Reynolds is her son. She lives in Dringhouses and her son lives in Bath. They are able to describe living conditions, poverty and health in this area, and tell how Dr Reynolds was the first Labour councillor for the Guildhall Ward.

Mrs Rene Sheard

Mary Irene (Rene) Wright was born in the Black Swan, Peasholme Green, in 1911 and then moved across the road to the Woolpack, where her father was landlord. She attended the Haughton School and Sunday School at St Saviour's. Mrs Sheard died in March 1995.

Mr George Squire

Mr Squire was born in 1925 in Haver Lane, and later moved to a greengrocer's in Carmelite Street. He now lives in Strensall and is a Master Builder. He remembers how everything seemed dark and grey compared to modern times, and yet it was a very sociable, 'self-help' community.

Mr Samuel Thompson

Mr Thompson was baptised at St Saviour's Church in 1921, where his parents had earlier been married, and he now lives in Huntington. He was the middle one of six children, attended Castlegate and Bedern schools and worked at Rowntrees for almost 50 years.

Mr Andy Waudby

Mr Waudby was born in Hungate in 1921 and now lives in Upper Poppleton. He remembers the street games, a popular feature of childhood, and has made modern-day equivalents, such as a marble toe rack from wood. He has led a very colourful life, and in the Second World War became a spy for the Chinese Army against Japan. He speaks fluent Chinese and has transformed his garden into a Chinese garden open to tourists. The proceeds are donated to charity.

Mr Ernest Webster

Mr Webster was born in Duke of York Street in 1901 and was a Blue Coat school boy. Despite the strict discipline he endured, he learnt many useful crafts there and afterwards entered into apprenticeship. He now lives in Tang Hall.

1

The Environment

In the early part of the twentieth century, the Hungate district was one of the poorest in York, and was likened to a rabbit warren, because so many houses were packed into such a small space. The inhabitants were victim to the dirt and grime of local industry, as well as the vile smells from slaughterhouses and chicory works. Their homes were dwarfed by the huge prison-like building of Leetham's Mill, which stood on the promontory of the Foss and dominated the skyline. The streets were subject to flooding and the houses in such a terrible state that eventually they had to be demolished in the 1930s.

Yet despite poverty, disease and deprivation, or perhaps because of these common enemies, the people who lived in the area testify to a strong community spirit, where neighbours cared about each other and shared what little they had. Often those who suffer together and share adversity have stronger connections than those who are more secure.

When the residents were relocated to spanking new council houses in Clifton, Tang Hall and other parts of the city, seeing electric lighting, bathrooms and indoor toilets for the first time, many of them still missed the old way of life. They longed for the sharing and the comradeship, and felt that this was lost for ever when Hungate was torn down.

The Parish

The parish itself formed roughly the shape of a square, bordering Aldwark, St Saviourgate (a rather more affluent street, though the many courts and yards which led off it were the opposite), part of Fossgate and the River Foss.

Mr Jack Birch sets the scene,

Stonebow as it exists at present was simply not there. To get from the Pavement to Heworth the main road was St Saviourgate, then approaching the end, you turned right into St Saviour's Place, then Peasholme Green.

The land to the south of St Saviourgate was approached two ways. From Peasholme Green, where there was a fairly large open area known as the Haymarket, or by Hungate. Apart from the industrial complex on the River Foss, of Leetham's Flour Mill, the rest of the area was full of run-down houses.

According to Mr Thompson,

As you came down Hungate, near St Saviour's Church, where the garage is, underneath there was supposed to be a passage through to York Minster. And I've actually stood there. I could take you to it now.

Mr Deighton remembers the transport,

The trams used to come down Whip-ma-whop-ma-gate, up St Saviourgate, then they had buses - they used to call 'em ramless, trackless because they was the same as trams but without the tracks. They was navy-blue and white, run by the corporation. They used to run by overhead electricity but they could steer where they wanted. The electrobus had a battery in it - it had to be charged up.

Mr Andy Waudby evokes the familiar smells of the area,

You had this mist off the river, and the smell was like chickweed, if you go to a stagnant pond anywhere you can smell it. I recognise it as soon as I smell it. Hungate. And then where Dan Parkin had his 'osses, so you get the smell off the manure heap. Now, to clean the drains out, Corporation used to bring a two-wheeled cart down. And you had the blokes with big poles, with half a box on the end; and they used to lift the grate up and used to scoop all the muck out into this thing. Now in summer the smell from those drains, it was like midnight in the Shambles. Talk about Eau de Cologne. Then you had the smell from the slaughterhouses. And you had the smoke and the smell from the gas works. Everybody was affected because when you had a foggy day you'd get smoke from all the chimleys.

On a Saturday you'd get this water tank on two wheels, and a Corporation bloke used to come with the 'oss and this tank, and pull a lever and at back there was like a pipe of water, a stream to keep the dust down. You could get more water by spitting on it.

Not all the houses in the parish were the same. The beauty and comparative grandeur of St Saviourgate contrasted sharply with the run-down tenements of Bedern. Mr Deighton describes Ebor Buildings in Bedern,

These was tenement flats, with a common staircase that used to be open at every floor and they used to live off them. And the kids that lived there were really down and out. They used to come to school with their shoes fastened round the neck and they only put the shoes on when they got to school, because Mr Cammidge wouldn't allow 'em into the school without shoes on.

There was only two rooms in some of them. And they was five or six kids to a family. But I can never remember any nastiness with the people in Bedern who were just poor, out of work, and through being out of work they was on the breadline. But you go round the corner into Aldwark and the people there all had good jobs. They worked at the railway, corporation, the brewery which was down there.

Mrs Fearn also remembers Ebor Buildings,

It was like in these old American films, the tenements. I had a friend that went to our school, that used to live in there and she was off ill. They asked me to call in and see her to find out what was matter with her. It was like being in a maze. I got frightened in the finish. I'd be about ten then. There was prams and cats and dogs, and rabbit hutches with rabbits in, on the landings. And I never found her.

Hungate was self-contained. You knew exactly where you were, no matter what alleyway you went in, what doorway you went through. And eventually, all you did was come out of it, into Fossgate or Pavement.

Mr Ted Chittock recalls the different types of housing,

There was a contrast between St Saviourgate on one side and the other because on the one side there was the doctors like Reynolds and he was a very good doctor, because I once had an accident on Centenary Chapel. I stuck a spike in me leg and we went across to Reynolds and he fixed it.

My sister lived in a garret where the steps was probably two feet across. And it spiralled up stone steps, up and off the landings was the rooms. And all those consisted of one room. Then there was St John's Place where I was born and that was off Haver Lane. Now those was the normal two up two down. The floor was quarry tiles. There was a front room and a backroom kitchen. The staircase led to the bedrooms. The fireplace was where you did all the cooking. It was a big black range with the old spit things over the top of it.

Then you had a contrast across the road, [St Saviourgate] where me sister moved into some years later, which was a big house, with a Georgian frontage and a balustraded staircase.

Brass Rapper Row [Carmelite Street] was a famous place, where all the row of houses had brass rappers. Every woman on a morning used to stone the steps. That's how proud they were of their homes. There was a house in Hungate what had a tree growing up through the front room of it - believe it or not.

When they started pulling it down they found a mysterious room, people had been complaining about for years, where there was knocking going on. And when they opened this room, it had obviously been an undertaker's. There was a cart in it, old chisels, and half-made coffins stuck up on the walls.

Mrs Reynolds lived in St Saviourgate but visited Bedern,

There was a passageway called Kendal's Passage and down the passage were lots of little cottages, and Mr Kendal used to come every morning, very big man, very tall, and he always wore a high hat and tails - one of the old school, and all these cottages belonged to him.

Because these places share an old sort of water tap. Like a pump in the middle of the yard, and this is where you'd see the little kids standing at the end, very often in bare feet.

In Bedern, they were absolutely terrible and they belonged to an alderman, and we were horrified to think that they lived in such opulence and these poor things...I can remember my husband telling me, 'Darling, you can't possibly be a conservative when things like that...You must come with me and I'll show you', and he took me round.

There was buckets of urine and everything else on the landings; there were no lavatories. Bare stairs too, I can remember that. No-one believed they lived in such a terrible state and I must say the people were really charming although they were suffering such poverty. In the olden days York was known as the three P's - poor, proud and pretty. Under the pretty side was the seamy side.

Mrs Sheard remembers,

There was one family of about thirteen people in one bedroom and one room downstairs. Off Haymarket there was a square of houses which went round into Brunswick Terrace. It was a big square, there was about twelve houses and they shared a communal yard at the back with one solitary grate for the slops. All these twelve houses, all the slops went down there and I think there was about half-a-dozen toilets at the very end of the yard.

Down Haver Lane, very very narrow little street. Tiny footpath at either side, and the families seemed to be brought up on the footpaths. In summer all the children, they were all outside because the little places they lived in were too small for 'em. They'd be overcrowded inside. But there always seemed to be crowds of children on the footpaths.

The Streets

Constant floods made the houses damp and there were rats, as Mr Deighton observes,

Talk about rats - whether they were water voles or not I don't know, but it was fair game for fellers to go ratting with the terriers on a Sunday morning and have bets, for every rat caught you got a penny. Everybody used to have a little terrier or a whippet.

Going down Layerthorpe, all those yards go down to the Foss. Whenever the Ouse used to flood, the Foss used to flood, and they all used to get covered in three or four feet of water in the houses.

Mrs Butterworth remembers the water coming very close,

It used to come up Garden Place. It's just high enough to get into the rooms. Standing on duckboards. We used to have about four gaslamps in Garden Place. Man used to come round.

There were some advantages as Mrs Fearn discovered,

Walkers coal yard was on Layerthorpe Bridge. It used to wash the coal out, and it used to come down in the water, and as it came past the bottom of Dundas Street, where the railings were, pieces used to come in through the railings, battered about, so you were sent out with a bucket and your bare feet, you didn't have wellies in those days. And you used to go collecting coal and take it back, used to dry 'em in front of the fire.

Although the floods left behind a terrible mess, the housewives still kept the streets as clean as they could, as Mrs Kay points out,

Floods in Lower Wesley Place, 1933

Stonebow Lane, which connected Hungate with Whip-ma-whop- ma-gate, was a yard wide. We had roadsweepers, but did our own, our mothers used to have us scrubbing the pavement, and the stone. You coloured your own steps. You did the part of your pavement where you lived, which was your little responsibility.

Mrs Butterworth's family were certainly house-proud,

Our yard was tarmac, but it was all broke, and we used to sweep it and then to stone round that cement round grates. With it being flats, it went up a passage, and there was two lots of stairs, one lot for your second floor and one lot for third and we used to stone the passage - make it nice and clean. There was never any rubbish knocking around like there is today. Always nice and clean curtains up, lace curtains.

Mr Burnett's too,

All you had was a big floor but it was spotlessly clean because the women used to get on their hands and knees and scrub it like hell. You could guarantee all the doorsteps in Garden Place and Hungate and that was always highly scrubbed, with carbolic soap and brush.

Garden Place, 1930s

The Houses

Mrs Butterworth describes the house she lived in:

There was just two rooms and one was kitchen. Toilet was outside. It was all rented down there. I don't think anybody had their own place. Well I think ours was about the only flats there was. And they did belong to Leetham's Mill. Everybody was overcrowded. There was ten of us. And she used to have two bedrooms in there so me mother had to partition the kitchen off...with curtains.

She tells how the families took pride in their homes, making sure they looked as neat and tidy as possible,

We had a lovely big York Range. Could see yourself through it. Blackleaded. Me dad used to do that. And we used to have a steel fender, and all stone floors. Bedroom was concrete. Kitchen was concrete, so was back-kitchen...used to do clip carpets did me dad. Everybody seemed to be comfortable.

We had a tap in the back kitchen. We had our own tap. Some had pumps, some had taps in the courtyard.

My mother always had a gas stove. But she just used that in summer time when she didn't want a fire on. She always baked in a fire oven, and she'd maybe do a stew on the fire, but she wouldn't fry on it. She used to fry on her stove. Then summer time to save your coal for winter, used to use your gas stove.

Mrs Alice Butterworth, 1995

Alice Butterworth and her husband, Garden Street, 1923

Mr Hall emphasises the pride that people had in their homes, despite the hard struggle to survive,

My dad died in France five days after the war started. There was seven of us children and we lived in two up two down and one little back yard and we had gas in our kitchen, little gas cooker. We got chance further away, it was two houses knocked into one, with four bedrooms. We had a great big yard but in that yard there was ever so many houses that had been half demolished and course there was no-one in them, but we had to go outside to our toilet and we had to take a light, it was so dark. For all them little houses were small, some of them were little palaces. Brass fenders, brass spittoons, everything brass.

Wally Holmes's mother, like most of the women, worked very hard to look after her family,

She used to go down [to the market] at eight o'clock Saturday night, we also used to go as well, under the vegetable stalls, stuffing stuff into bags, vegetables, fruit and everything else there, and mother used to shop there. She'd get a piece of meat, weighed about two stone at least and that was our Sunday joint. And then sandwiches right up to Thursday or so, the following week. And how they kept stuff fresh and such like I don't know but you did, because all that was over it, was a small-meshed net.

We were rich in everything else, young, how everybody mixed and kept together. Mother had to come home from market last thing and then after that she'd set off and mix the dough. Big earthenware dish, then she'd put the cloth over it and leave it in the fireplace all night...on the Yorkish range. It'd stop there all night to ferment. Then she must've got up at least eight o'clock on Sunday morning there, 'cos when we got up, our back yard was absolutely full of bread cakes, bread rolls and the smell of fresh bread and we had warm bread cakes for breakfast. We used to look forward to that.

I'll never forget me mother one time and it stands out in my mind. She were baking and mixing and this was summertime and some caraway seed had got into the dough and whether it were one of us that knocked it into it or what but

me mother carried the whole lot, a big hunk of it, down to the Foss and heaved it over the edge.

Mrs Kay recalls her house:

We had the old horse-hair sofa, old rocking chair, a chest of drawers and it was bow-fronted - and it had four big drawers and two little ones, we had a sideboard and then in the kitchen it was just a table and chairs. There was a coal fire in the front, with gas lighting, lots and lots of ornaments. I remember once me mother opened a drawer and it was absolutely full, running all over the place. Blackbeetles. But we kept a dog and a cat.

Down Hungate you went down like a kind of passage and it opened out into a square, and there were communal toilets and a big standpipe in the middle - like a concrete pillar with just one tap, and I would say about fifteen houses shared that one tap. I think they were paved round the houses and cobbled stones in the middle.

Hungate Wide Yard, 1930s

Andy Waudby's house was similar,

The women used to scrub the steps. They would perhaps put pottery mould on the steps, like a bar of soap and you rub it on and it comes out purple white.

Then you used to get like a yeller block, like limestone and rub that on. I used to ask why they always scrubbed the steps, and I learnt that it was to keep the devil away. And that's where it sort of originated from.

Now a lot of houses in Hungate you could walk right off the street into the house. You'd have a chest o'drawers, a table in the middle, and a sofy.

On the mantelpiece you'd get pot dogs, or pot horses. Then the old range. You'd have a piece of material on the mantelpiece, hanging down, with fringes, tassels on sometimes. Then candlesticks and the ornaments. My grandmother used to polish them every Friday.

Gaslighting in the centre of the room. Now being poor, you're lucky if you could afford a mantle. And you put it on, and it was like a piece of netting. And you put it on very gently, turn it to the right a little bit on two lugs. And this held it up. Then you'd get a match and light it and it used to flare up, and then it would go black a little bit, like sooty. And then it got hotter and hotter. Once you'd lit it, you just had to touch it or knock it, once you got hold of it, it just disintegrated.

Upstairs, you'd get a brass bedstead. Metal struts each side of the bed. So we've got brass at top here and a brass end with railings and brass knobs on. That's where you get the saying 'with brass knobs on'.

Then we have a mattress...full of straw...about six inches wide. It was a good flea breeder, bug breeder. Then you had your sheets, if you were lucky you had sheets, if not you had a blanket. You couldn't afford a mantle upstairs, so all you had was a gas jet. Candles were good for burning fleas; specially bugs, cremate 'em.

And then you'd have a washing stand...with a wash bowl stuck in it. Nearly all the houses had a big jug and a bowl. They were small rooms, you couldn't swing a cat about in 'em.

So you'd have the women all helping the little ones here, and as they got older they go higher up the stairs. They'd be sat there eating on the stairs. Time and time again you'd go into houses where a little lass or a lad had died of meningitis - it's nothing fresh to go in t'room and see a coffin on the clean table cloth.

You always smelt of carbolic soap. The women's clothes were clean, the children were clean. Clean at morning, but by tea time looked as if they'd been up bloody chimney. But I think to meself the womenfolk, they had a lot on their plate. Must have been a hard life, as hard as it was for the men in the flour mills and gas works.

Mrs Thompson recalls that,

Nearly all houses was just an up and a down and one bedroom, you was lucky if you had two. And the toilets was duckets. I mean you could have...gone through your own door to the toilet, but you could have shook hands with one in next to you, 'cos it was a long line went along.

And Mr Thompson explains that,

Toilet paper was newspaper torn up into squares and fastened on with a bit of string. No fancy stuff for us.

Mr Deighton's brother,

used to live down Brunswick Place and he used to have two rooms upstairs and two down. Share a toilet with another ten houses. The yard was so slippery with soap, throwing soap water down it and it used to go into one drain, the suds. It was like a layer of soap and I stood on it - whoosh! Straight across the yard and banged me head, cried for a week.

Some houses had a 'best room' like Mrs Cook's,

We had a front parlour used on special occasions, red plush chesterfield and chairs. One with horsehair was in the living room. Dad used to play piano and there was a big aspidistra.

Mrs Aldrich lived in Webster's Passage,

There was no back way, there was just a front entrance, and it was a very long living room and adjoining that was another room, where you did cooking and that. Then adjoining that was what we used to call the Far Spot. It was all in one, one length.

And there was really plenty of room in it, but no facilities at all, but we had a coal fire which we did baking with, and there wasn't hot or cold water.

I used to bake for my mother from maybe twelve years old, used to help her. We had a fire cooker. Bars was in middle, then there was a little ledge either side where you could put your pans. It was really a queer looking oven, used to open out more like a range.

Mrs Fearn,

had the one living-room-kitchen, off Dundas Street and a little kitchen at the back of that. And a little backyard.

We had a copper. Father used to burn anything. It was like being on an Indian reservation. When he used to want to get it going in winter. There was a couple of taps in the middle so everybody used to go out and get their water from the middle there.

You're straight in and up the stairs, then you were straight into your living room. A nice big fireplace and a mantelpiece, tassels on your cover over the mantle, and always a fender, stainless steel and a Tidy Betty, which was a thing that went in front of the fire itself so the ashes wouldn't come out on to the hearth.

Then there was your fire and this just went round in front, kept that, had to be well brassed and everything. And an oven at the side of the fire. Used to have a big pan that you used to boil your washing in, on the top of the fire, sheets and pillow cases and things like that, were boiled in that pan.

That was all in the one room, and there was another door you went in and we'd a little tiny kitchen, and there was a sink in there, a stone sink, and nothing else. We eventually had a gas cooker put in there.

Mrs Nellie Fearn, 1995

Mrs Greenley lived in,

A little two bedroomed house in Spen Lane. Five of us kids and me mam, who was 28, lived there. We shared a toilet with next door, at end of the yard and had to take buckets to put water down. Mother had to work anyway she could, she did ironing for Dr Reynolds, ironed his shirts, and cleaning at Ross's fish shops. We had to sleep four girls in one room and the lad in the other. Me mam on the sofa.

Nellie Goodwin, Dundas Street, 1934

Used to clean up in evenings, Mother made us all brush our hair for a long time. Friday night was paraffin night in case of nits, we put it on and then washed it off.

Not only were the houses small but the area itself was gloomy, as Mr Squire explains,

The living conditions were very bare. I remember them putting electric light in the shop on Carmelite Street. There was one cold tap and if you wanted water to get a bath, you used to boil it. You used to sit in the short bath on a Friday night in the front room...everybody got bathed, used the same water. In the terrace you had two bedrooms upstairs and one fire in the house and that was the range. When you went to bed you bloody froze. You never slept in the sheet, you got in the blanket because the blanket was warm. The floors were flagged, we had pricked rugs in front of the fire. If they were all out I used to get a cat out of the street and catch mice 'cos the whole place was running with mice and

George Squire, with his grandfather's watch, 1995

George Squire and his grandfather, Have Lane, 1927

there were rats outside with it being a mill. Used to set 'em in the corners where rubbish had been dumped.

We had ordinary chairs and settee when we had the shop. Dad bought it for half a crown and covered it himself with imitation leather. And a sideboard and a Marconi radio. Life was dreadfully hard in the 30s. It was very grey and drab everywhere, nothing in the streets, you'd see people on bikes and there was one car that came in Haver Lane and that was my uncle Charlie. He had an open top Chevy with a running board like Al Capone.

You never saw flowers. Bats used to fly around by gaslight. Everything was grey and dark, nothing bright. Never saw white shirts, always striped thick stuff, flannelette with no collars, flat caps and scarf round the necks. My grandfather had a homburg. The men wore working boots but my Dad used to wear shoes.

The only clothes you had were two pair of trousers, a vest, a shirt and a coat, a pair of boots or shoes or if things were bad, black plimsolls. We had to take cash clothing check, paid something every week.

But I think the worst thing of all were the blackclocks. When you turned the light out and if you come round and struck a match, the floor would be covered in blackclocks. You could smell them.

St Saviourgate was very different from the poorer areas of the parish, and Mr Cave's home was in that street,

Our house was in a block of four and at the top of the last storey was attics, divided into two on one side of the house and two on the other and you go through from one attic to the other because it sloped way right back. Cats used to walk along the tiles. My bedroom was in the attic on the top floor. There was five flights of stairs...and cellars underneath. The coal people used to come and on the pavement there used to be a square piece of iron on a chain and they used to lift it up, empty the bags of coal in the main street and put it back again.

My father was manager of an advertising business called Sheldons and they had bottom floor as offices and workshops. Had eleven rooms in the house. Had one room called best room upstairs. On either side of the fireplace you pulled levers and a bell rang in the passageway.

Mrs Law lived in a shop in St Saviourgate during the late 1940s and 50s,

Ours was a Georgian house with cellar, ground floor, first floor, second floor and an attic. Lovely big rooms and old staircase. We used to run up and down and slide down banisters. The back yard was on two levels, full of flowers, Mum bought flowers every Saturday in the market. She put them into any kind of container she could find, and into the garden. We didn't have a back entrance so dustbins had to come through the house on Friday mornings.

When we first went there was a great big fireplace with black leading, brass handles and an oven at the side. It was in for two or three years, we didn't use it for cooking but put our pyjamas in there at night to warm them ready for bed. One day, the door was open and the cat got in and when we opened it to put pyjamas in, it shot out. Fortunately it was all right. There was a door at the side of the fire which led to a little room under the stairs with a sloping roof, we put washing on clothes horses in there to dry.

Further down the street on the same side as the church was a lovely double-fronted house. The daughter had a pony and kept it in the garden until she found somewhere to keep it. She had to take the pony through the house for about a month. There was an enormous garden with tennis court and vegetable plot, rose arches, and a big lawn.

We all had our own jobs. On a Sunday I used to start at the top of the house and dust and polish all the way down. The sitting room wasn't used that often and one Sunday it smelt damp so I put the electric fire on, to leave it on for a couple of hours and closed the door and forgot about it. The following Sunday when I worked my way down and opened the sitting room door, the heat just hit me. The electric fire had been left on the whole week. I daren't tell Mum but I plucked up courage to tell her and all she said was 'Never mind, it's had a good airing'.

Jack Birch also lived in the same street yet he did not escape some of the problems which affected those in Hungate itself,

Number 29 is a tall, Georgian house. My father was very fond of it 'cos I remember the first floor, it was taken up by a drawing room, parallel with the street, which had a rather ornate cornice in it. Being a Georgian building there were lots of nooks and crannies, and I remember mother was very disturbed because we had a plague of blackclocks - rain beetles.

You know they're about an inch in length - and we had a special gadget to trap these beasts. It was a type of open bowl in the centre of which was a small cup which held a liquid to attract the beetles. They proceeded to come up the sides of this apparatus, and when they got on to the portion of rods that supported the centre-piece, there was a two sided flap and if they got slightly out of balance this tipped and dropped the beetles into some poisonous liquid in the bowl. Mother used to catch large numbers of beetles that way.

Jack Birch, 1995

Today, St Saviourgate is not very different from its earlier self, but much of the surrounding area was condemned as 'unfit for human habitation' and so had to be demolished between 1933 and 1938. A great many houses were razed to the ground and their inhabitants re-housed. One lady remembers that,

When Hungate was taken down, there were so many rats around that the Corporation shovelled them onto carts to be taken away and gassed.

Stonebow, a wide street built in 1960, cut Hungate in two. Stonebow House, most of which is a multi-storey car park, is widely considered to be York's ugliest building. So the new streets and buildings which replaced the demolished area were no improvement.

When families were moved to new housing in Clifton and other parts of York, it was quite an upheaval. To begin with, all the houses' contents had to be removed, as Mr Thompson witnessed,

In them days they used to bring a big van and put all your furniture in it and what they call fumigate it, get rid of all the bugs. They took all the stuff on a night time in this van. Everybody had these bugs, it was no good trying to say you hadn't.

Mr Chittock continues the story,

Then they took it to Foss Islands and they connected it up and they fumigated the whole of that van. So that when you went into your new house there was no danger of anything.

The difference between Hungate and the new council houses was enormous. Mrs Kay recalls,

going to the house in Peterhill Drive. And we just had nothing, and we just had to wait while the van came. What I remember is, we all got into trouble because when we'd got light bulbs we all went mad - running round and round

Stonebow House, 1995

putting switches on. My mother said, 'If you don't leave them alone it's gonna cost me money'.

For many residents the move was a traumatic experience, which took years to come to terms with. Perhaps some never have. Mrs Butterworth echoes many others when she says, "Wish I was there now, I do, I wish I lived there now."

2

A Child's Eye-View

In the Hungate area, children spent much of their life outside. There was no television, and no-one could afford to buy toys, so they had to improvise, sometimes in unusual ways as Mrs Sheard points out,

When I was a kid, I was always with my dad and we used to go down to the cellar to relieve the mice from the traps. There was tons of mice there. And of course they were all dead, and I used to put all these dead mice, every morning, into me doll's pram, and if it was a wet day, I used to wrap 'em up in Wright's polony skin, and they were me babies. And the next day I used to get some new 'uns and chucked 'em out.

Andy Waudby found out how to make the best kind of weapon,

At the bottom of Coppergate you had Hooks...fishing tackle, guns, you could buy a catapult there if you wanted one. Mind you we used to make 'em. Used to get elastic off lasses, off their drawers. You can't beat a good home made one.

Mrs Law's mother,

had an old fox fur cape that she hadn't worn for years, in a wardrobe in the attic and once we put it on a piece of string and dangled it out of the window when people walked past.

Children did not often play games at home, but congregated in the streets, like Mrs Kay and her friends,

The girls just played around the streets. Whatever season, if it was skipping time we all used to skip, you have a long length of rope, we got two girls, one at

Dundas Street, 1930s

each end and we'd all take it in turns to wind, or if you were lucky you got your own. Played whip and top, any old bicycle wheel we could get hold of and we use to bool that up and down the streets with a stick.

Wally Holmes also enjoyed these street games, though the boys tended to be rather more adventurous,

We used to have what we called winder smashers. It was like a top with a long stem, like a mushroom. When you whipped a thing round there, that really went and many a time your string wrapped round it and it didn't spin your top, it picked it up and slung it and you heard somebody's winder go. You was off.

Sometimes they ventured a little further afield, like Mrs Kay,

One of our playgrounds was the Bar Walls, just on St Maurice's Road. On Foss Islands....where the iron bridge is that goes over the Foss, there was a canal there, a concrete outcome and there was warm water coming out of there and we all went paddling, till the policeman caught us - he used to give us a good clip.

And we also used to go on Navigation Road, before those flats were built. We used to take a little picnic, of bread and jam and bottles of water.

We used to play in Whip-ma-whop-ma-gate...there used to be an iron bar across, right in the corner and we played there for hours, swivelling round this iron bar.

Mr Waudby played in the water at Foss Islands, until he had a nasty experience,

The coppers used to chase us there... we used to run like hell over this asphalt. I don't know why we didn't cut our feet. The last time I went swimming in there, there were two or three of us, and there was a bag floating about in the water, and it had got jammed up near the power station, because at the side they had some square thing, a wooden platform on concrete. I think it was where the intake pipes were for the water for generating. These blokes picked this bag out and they split open and there was a dead pig in, and it was all green and it was a fortnight after, all my face broke out and I had an awful face, for a few weeks. I never went swimming there again. That was my last experience of swimming in the Foss.

Samuel Thompson also knew the place,

They used to gamble on Pound Garth, tossing tuppence and they'd get raided by the police and they'd jump in the Foss, swim down t'Foss and get out of it down there. It wasn't very deep. There was a little bridge near the cooling tower and we used to swim there. There were all reeds. We used to say, 'Are you going bare golly?'"

There was a keen interest in sport, and Reg Deighton and his friends,

used to play football in Spen Lane. Ball used to go over the top 'cos we used to climb over the big boards to go in. There used to be a slope, and the lads used to play king of the slope, and we'd to get up there and you had to pull everybody down. Of course we used to wear galoshes or plimsolls as they're called now. Jean Bell was the prettiest girl in the street, she lived in Aldwark actually, and she knocked me feet from under me, didn't try to push, just knocked me feet, and that was it, I was knocked off. And I fell down and I just punched her one, straight in the nose. And it bled all over. Of course she went home and told her mother, her mother told the school, and the next morning at assembly, the headmaster called me out and give me three on each hand. I couldn't cry but I was really humiliated. And I've never struck a woman since!

Many children did not have a football. Andy Waudby,

went to the slaughterhouse in Hungate and asked for a pig's bladder. We blew it up and played football. We couldn't afford a rugby ball so we made a parcel of old newspapers and used that.

Mr Cave,

played on St George's Field - cricket, football. We must have worn the grass away. Used the trunk of a tree for wickets, used to mark it with a chalk. Used to be St George's baths, we knocked a ball right through t'window.

Andy Waudby certainly found plenty of things to keep him amused,

Did you know there was once a lion escaped down Lady Peckitt's Yard? Years ago they had a...circus..in Parliament Street where the market was and one of the lions escaped and it ran a-ruddy-mok there. And that's where they collared it, in Lady Peckitt's Yard.

When I was a lad there was Black Harry and his gunboat - the River King. That's where I learned to...scull, on one o't cocky boats of the barges. We built a canoe...in the house. It was too big, we couldn't get it through the door, so we had to take it to pieces again. Eventually... we got it down to Leeman Road, this kid George and me started paddling up river, bloody thing sank.

And there was the time we used to sit and watch the Blackshirts and wait for them to start fighting. And when they started fighting on the floor, the money used to come out of their pockets. We used to sit there and just watch them.

Then the meat wagon used to come - the Black Maria from the police - after they'd scattered we'd go and look for the money that had spilt.

Mr Squire, too, found other means of entertainment,

I saw a wake in Stonebow passage, Finnegan Brothers took me down and the coffin was propped up down there. The corpse had a hat and brown suit and big boots, and the women were drinking gin out of mugs.

Mrs Cook and her friends, pursued more gentle interests. They

played with marbles and cigarette cards. We'd pretend to make scent with rose petals and water in a bottle and shake it up.

But some of the girls were mischievous, like Mrs Thompson,

We'd gone into t'churchyard, playing. And they shouted, 'hey up, there's vicar coming'. I was a bit chubbier than the others, they all fell over the railings and my elastic of my knicker legs caught on it and pulled me back, and spike stuck right though my leg. They had to lift me off and take me to hospital. And I had two stitches but then I got a good hiding on top for being in.

In the early 1950s, when Hungate had been demolished, Mrs Law would play on the open ground,

When it was light nights we used to go on our bikes onto Hungate, which was derelict, hills, soil, it was all rubble, shrubs and trees. It was BMX type thing but we had ordinary bikes and we'd go crashing up and down these hills and we'd always be getting punctures.

Sometimes entertainers would liven up the streets. Mrs Fearn remembers several of them,

You got an old chap and he used to sing, O ta-rat-a-ta. Then there was Burlington Bertie - he used to stroll down with his top hat and his coats and do the lot. And then this old man who come with his concertina and he used to play

it and all the time he was playing it he used to go hu, hu, hu; you could never hear what he was playing, because he was huhuing all the time.

When you used to come out you used to say, 'Where are we going to stand outside tonight? Where do you think best fight'll be?' You used to think you were lovely when you were fourteen or fifteen in those days. Go round and got talking to boys and they'd say, 'Where do you live?' And we never used to tell them we lived in Hungate, or they would say, 'That's where they play tiggy with hammers'. But it was a great atmosphere.

Occasionally there would be other special forms of entertainment, like the fair on Haymarket, though this was not without its dangers, as Mrs Sheard found out,

The cocks and horses went right round outside our house. My mother had a fit once - I was outside on these swings and horses, and somebody went in to me mam, 'Oh, Mrs Wright, there's a man taken your Rene down the yard'. Course she was up in arms and me dad was right there, and this man was a married man, he lived in Orchard Street. He had eight or nine children of his own, and he'd picked a bairn up. My dad got him though, he was caught running away.

For some children, there was the summer outing to look forward to, and Mrs Kay was lucky enough to go,

They came round and they got the names of poor children. So we had our name down, and on the day of the trip we had to go to the cattle market. And that was round where the Barbican Baths is now, and there was double-decker buses - I don't know who organised it - I suppose maybe some charity or something. We had to go in lines of two, and to keep us all in order we were all fed into the cattle pens...it was just like a snake going round. And as you got on the bus - you were given a brown bag with an apple and an orange and a sandwich and a penny. And we went to Filey...It was the highlight of the year.

Wally Holmes also remembers such trips,

The favourite place was Hunmanby Gap. And there we had our dinner. And it was allus Wright's sausage rolls, Wright's pork pies. Which was given by Wright's freely to poor children of York.

Sunday Schools also organised outings and Mrs Aldrich went along,

Reverend Smith was the vicar of St Saviour's Church. And he organised a party of us to go by bus to Filey for the day. We got a penny, and then we got ice-cream when we got there. We had a right good time on t'beach.

For Mrs Butterworth, it was the country rather than the sea,

Used to go to the Band of Hope and Sunday School down a passage there, that was our Hungate mission. If we went out on a Sunday we'd generally go on Clifton Ings, round Homestead, we never got no farther. And the Sunday School trip on horse and carts to Stockton Hall.

Mr Thompson recalls,

If you went on t'Sunday School outing they'd take you on a horse and cart. They'd wash it down, put a couple of sacks on and go as far as Strensall Common. Give you a bag of buns and I had my catapult. Good day out. It was brilliant for us 'cos we had nothing at all. Centenary Chapel was that.

George Squire knew one family who had eighteen children,

It was the first time they'd seen sausage and eggs, when the missionaries gave them breakfast. There was a Poor Boys' Trip to Scarborough and the Salvation Army had parties, there was no fighting because all everyone did was eat.

Mrs Greenley remembers other trips,

Once a year the coalman would take so many kids for a ride in the country for a 'holiday' and picked out a few. Put newspaper down to sit on. I went only once. Used to go to Homestead though, on Sunday afternoon. Practise the Maypole.

I got made May Queen at Homestead. Had long hair to my waist, and my mother washed and frizzed it.

Mrs Law and her sister also enjoyed days away,

As we got older, we went to the youth club at Centenary Chapel. When we were younger we went there for Sunday School on Sunday afternoons and on trips. My mum couldn't go on trips because of the shop so other people had to look after me and my sister. We had to go dressed alike so if one of us got lost, they knew what to look for.

Others were happy enough to take a trip across York, like Mrs Hall, who

used to go on the tram to Knavesmire and there was a band there. We made daisy chains and wore white shoes and socks and we were all right until we walked into cow dirt.

Andy Waudby got taken on trips, but for him it wasn't much fun,

I might as well a' stopped at home, because we'd go to a pub, soon as you got to Scarborough. We'd go to Scarborough for the day and I used to stand outside while my dad went into the pub, and I'd stand there, wait for him and he'd give me an ice-cream cornet and after an hour or so he'd come out. We used to go on the beach for ten minutes, sit on t'sand. We'd go and get fish and chips then back to the pub and move to the next pub.

He had a better time staying in York,

During the summer holidays we would take potato sacks and make tents with sacks and brush shafts on York racecourse, and played Cowboys and Indians.

An old soldier befriended him and took him fishing,

We couldn't afford a rod so he taught me to make one and make a float out of birds' feathers. The man brought broken biscuits and peanuts for us both and we spent hours fishing. He taught me to live by a saying, which later helped me

to get through and save my life in Burma. It was, 'Never let it be said that your mother bred a quitter'.

Pound Garth

One of the few places which was recognised as a children's playground was Pound Garth, where the present-day Ambulance Station is situated. Wally Holmes considered it very important,

Pound Garth was a regular meeting place for all Hungate. They all was there playing this, playing that. But the big main thing was tiggy exxy. I should imagine the exxy bit is getting rid of the ball. When you'd been tug, the ball must exit, get rid of it. It was rugby in a way, what they call, union men, touch rugby. Soon as you touch, pass. Well they were on there, they used to come

The site of Pound Garth, 1995

until there'd be maybe twenty a side in t'finish. Especially when the gamblers were playing as well. Pitch and toss club, they had lookouts planted. As soon as the flat-feet were coming, they all knew then, look out - at signal - to join in playing tiggy exxy. And then when police went away, back they went again and carried on with their pitch and toss.

Reg Deighton played on Pound Garth,

Bedern School used to use it as their playing field and we used to have our annual gala when we had races. But mainly we used to go down there on a summer's night and play cricket with a hard ball, and stumps knocked in. We would play tiggy-exxy, but instead of playing with a rugby ball we used to roll brown paper up tight, fasten it with string until it was about ten inches long and four inches circumference, and we used to use that. There was some good players came out of there, for York Rugby League, and Jacky Linfoot, he played for Great Britain, in the first amateur rugby league side that went to Australia. There used to be some really rough games played there. My brother was the captain and they won the cup, and I was a little lad and I was sat on his shoulders, holding the cup on his head, and we went round Layerthorpe and Hungate, and everywhere challenging them that we'd won the cup.

Mrs Hall remembers it too,

We used to call it Hungate park. If we'd any games on from school, rounders or anything, we used to go there. We had swings and see-saw and sand, spend many an hour down there. In them days, little simple things you enjoyed. I had some friends that had a greengrocer's shop and we used to sit on the pavement playing jacks. Four little square jacks and you'd a ball, you put the four jacks down and you'd bounce the ball and you'd pick one up until you got four and then in the finish you had to throw the ball up and catch that and get all the four and if you did that, you won. Shuttlecocks and battledore on Shrove Tuesday, and lads had whips and tops, and also played hopscotch with a shiny piece of stone. If you got a crate of oranges from the shop and they were fastened up with band and it was plaited, we used to use that for skipping rope.

But part of Pound Garth was private property, owned by Mr (Daddy) Dowson, as Mr Deighton recalls,

He had all sorts in there, he used to have a few hens, and a pig. If you went in there you went at the risk of being chased by a dog or hit by him with a stick. And of course if you went home, you couldn't say to your dad, 'Daddy Dowson hit me with a stick', 'cos all you got was, 'You shouldn't have been in his place'.

The private area did not stop the children going in, as Mrs Fearn explains,

It was a proper park. We used to go picnicking there. It had cinders underneath but there was grass there as well. And railed off, but the boys used to break in - the girls as well.

Andy Waudby was one of them,

And then we used to make our kite and fly it there. But Daddy Dowson's had this wooden fence, and we used to climb over ruddy top, then we discovered if we got a saw, and sawed some of the railing out, then we could squeeze through that way.

Samuel Thompson remembers,

This used to be one side, they used to have their gang, and on the other side there was Pound Garth where the electricity works is now. They'd make a bonfire on the other side and one on Pound Garth and they used to go raiding and pinch it off one another. Pound Garth was ours. We did have fun, there was mischief, but no vandalism. You'd sooner help people.

Mrs Kay had another incentive,

It was like a little orchard. We used to go raid his trees, some of his apples...and he'd see us and he'd have the police round. If Kipperfeet caught you, you'd get a slap round the ear.

The two policemen who are best remembered were known as Kipperfeet and Galoshagob. They were respected by the children, and Reg Deighton explains why,

They used to give instant punishment. You got a clout round the ear, and if you ran away, they used to carry a cape and whack, it used to hurt. And there used to be a police box in Peasholme Green and if you wanted a policeman and he wasn't there, there was a little box you could pick the telephone up and speak to Clifford Street. And they used to put a blue light that used to flash, on top. The policeman'd be walking around or on his bike, and as soon as he saw that, he'd go to the box. They were very secretive, you never got inside the premises, they used to always keep the door shut. But you knew when they was in.

And nearly all the policemen...used to play rugby for York. I think there was three or four big policemen down there.

Ted Chittock also recalls the policemen,

We used to call him Galoshagob. You didn't mess about with him because in those days a policeman had a leather cape and he had a lion's head on either side of a chain that joined it up. If you was in any trouble, he'd just whip you like that, and you felt that lion's head. But they was the law and that was it. And you respected them for it.

The MP for York became Governor of Bengal or Bombay or somewhere like that. They used to come round in motor cars and they used to let us ride on the backs of them, or running boards. Vote Vote Vote for .... and you can't vote for a better man. And then the next day when they announced it from the Mansion House steps, who got in, we used to go looking at the cars and the policemen says, 'Hoppit!'. You could do what you liked when you were going round shouting and singing for electioneering, but you look at that car afterwards, they thought you were going to steal it.

Mrs Fearn knew that you didn't mess with the law,

I remember one winter's night, and this was snowing, been snowing like mad.

And it was on a slope, down off Haymarket. Used to love to go down the slides. And we were doing the slides, and Betteridge came, great big chap, and he made us, go on, get away. And he went into this little shop, and he bought this salt, and he started putting it on t'slides. Some of the lads started pelting him with snowballs, knocked his hat off and he went for them. Everybody scarpered. And my brother wasn't quick enough and he got him. And he knocked on our door and me dad answered, and he said, 'Now then, what's he been doing?' So he told him. So me dad says to him, 'Hast thou clipped his ear?', 'I haven't touched him, Harry'. He says, 'Thee clip one ear, and when I get him inside, I'll clip t'other'.

Mr Thompson recalls,

You saw all the policemen 'cos they were on foot, but you had your own bobby and he knew all your names. And he'd say 'I'll tell your mother of you.' Never your father! And you'd get a good hiding there.

Andy Waudby was more sceptical about the police, believing that they were not keen on Hungate children,

We were poor. And they were all for the rich, the well off. And the poor had to suffer. If you were poor, God help you. But if you've money and influence, you were all right.

So if you get a lad who comes from a well off family and he was caught committing something, and you got a lad from the poor part, the poor lad would get the book thrown at him.

You'd get a good hiding for stealing and to cheek somebody you'd get a good hiding. You'd get a kick up the backside and a bat over the ear'ole.

Now I've been on top of a tram, with kids going to see the football, up at Fulford. And a lady would get on and they'd stand and let the lady sit down. These are lads out of Hungate. Scruffy lads with their backsides hanging out, snotty nosed, angels with dirty faces.

Andy and two of his friends managed to get into the church choir and he felt very proud to be a choirboy,

until people complained about our haircut and threw us out. I felt sure the Lord did not mind our haircut but the snobs did.

Not everyone respected the police as Mrs Sheard points out,

There was one certain person, on Haymarket, she liked a drink. Then she'd quarrel with anybody. The police were always there Saturday nights. She'd go upstairs, and ... emptied the water closet on the coppers' heads. 'Get out, yer so and so's, get away, clear off.' She really was a nice person, but when she'd had a few, she'd row with her own shadow.

There were some special occasions for children during the year, and the most important was Christmas. Mrs Butterworth,

used to get orange and apple, a few nuts and a new penny, a bit of Christmas cake and a bit of cheese wrapped up and that was our Christmas stockings. But we thought as much about 'em as what they do now - all these toys and things.

Mrs Kay enjoyed it too,

They really had Christmas. People had parties and for us children, we just did hang one of me dad's socks up, and in the toe of the stocking there was always a shiny threepenny bit. And there was an apple and an orange, a brand new hankie, which was beautiful and a bit of tinsel on top. As regards our family, there was three of us, me mum used to say - one year it's your Christmas, the next year it's your Christmas - and that person got a big toy. But the other two had to make do with the stocking. And the next year it was the other one's turn and they got a present, but they always kind of managed to get a present everybody else could use so you really weren't left out. If it were a pair of roller skates, everybody used them. Christmas cake time, we all had to freeze to death while the Christmas cake was cooking in the oven. She really had it off to a T, did my mum. She'd build the fire up, get it to a temperature - all by guesswork - and she'd mix the old Christmas pud. We all had a stir and nobody dare move in the house. We was all banned from the kitchen, we were all made to go into the other room. And nobody dared even open the door in case it altered the heating of the fire. Big sighs of relief when me mother said, 'it's finished', and that was done solely in the fire oven.

Mrs Lavinia Kay, with old flat iron, 1995

Mrs Aldrich remembers Bonfire Night in Hungate,

We used to collect what we could, put it on one great big bonfire, and have little sparklers. We collected 'em up and shared them, as far as they would go round.

A great big bonfire it was, I don't know whether it was where Rieveley's had their hay...a bit of spare ground there. Somewhere about the middle part of Hungate.

Mrs Kay also had a good time,

Lavinia Lawson with mother and sister, Haymarket, 1932

There was always a bonfire on the park - and there was always one down Garden Place - round through Garden Street and what went into a square. They weren't very big ones. Nobody was afraid of fireworks in those days. You were lucky, you got a dozen, and bangers, and your parents just give you matches and you just let them off. I can't recall anybody getting burnt by them.

Pancake Day. I mean that was really a day was that. Everybody had the pancakes. And maybe some of the streets would have a party. We did in our little street. They used to bring their own tables out and set them down the middle of the street, and all the kids would sit and the mums would come out with the frying pan with the big pancake in, tipping them out.

There were some organised activities, as Mrs Aldrich recalls,

Lads used to go to Scouts and we used to go to Girl Guides. There was a building at bottom more or less in Spen Lane, and we went back way to that, some sort of big church. It faced St Saviourgate.

And Mr Cave,

went to St Saviour's Church because it was across the road, but went to Boys' Brigade at Centenary Chapel. I didn't actually join Boys' Brigade, I had a short spell and got a bit cheesed off with the discipline. Used to have a belt and a round pork pie hat. Very popular, more than the Scouts, who had their HQ in St Saviourgate.

Many of the young boys in the area were able to join the Boys' Club off Hungate, and enjoy different activities there. It was run by the Hungate Mission and offered a gym, billiard and games room, a dramatic room, woodwork and handicrafts rooms.

Mr Squire can remember, "the Prince of Wales, who became King Edward, opening the Boys' Club and coming down in a big car."

Mrs Kay also saw the event,

I remember him coming plain as day, as though it was yesterday, and he was stood there and he had a black coat on, with a black astrakhan collar, and a black astrakhan hat. I remember him cutting the tape. But us girls wasn't allowed to go in because it was a boys' club.

Someone who did go to the club was Mr Ted Chittock,

There used to be a big place what they called the Hungate Adult School. And people, the adults, used to go up and get educated. But they changed this into the York Boys' Club. It started with a Sheffield Wednesday player who was crippled, called Joe Harrison. Now people who backed the York Boys' Club, was Noel Terry, from Terrys, Harris who was chairman of Rowntrees in those days, and Lumley-Dodsworth's two daughters from Bishopthorpe. There was prominent people who put money into it, and we had a massive gymnasium upstairs, boxing, everything. We even put plays on. We had a fantastic time. I remember the last one we did, with me brother and I. We was the bad men in the 'Babes in the Wood'.

Now that was the focus of everything in Hungate. I believe you had to be thirteen years of age to belong to the boys' club. And it was a very good thing because, although as I say, I don't think there was much crime in Hungate, but you tended as children to get into scrapes where the police was brought down and in those days there was nothing like going and complaining to the Chief Constable or anything like that about the policemen, because your mother would take you aside and give you another bat if you'd done something wrong. It was as bad as that.

The Boys' Club brought up a lot of boxers. One of the main instructors there was a man called Boy Watson. He used to work at Rowntrees and was a good boxer and a gentleman. I remember in those days the men fighting was Joe Routledge and another man called Harry Ainsworth. They was always on the bill of fighting. And invariably Joe won. He was a very, very good boxer. Come the war, Joe went straight in, was captured at Dunkirk, escaped from the prisoner of war camp to Switzerland and got back home again. Joe...died a few years ago...he worked at the carriage works with us, and was the nicest man you could wish to meet.

3

Schooldays

There were several schools in the parish at this time. Some Hungate children attended Bilton Street School in Layerthorpe, others went to Castlegate School, one or two even ventured further afield to Fishergate. The Blue Coat School in Peasholme Green (St Anthony's Hall, now the Borthwick Institute) was in a category of its own. But the two most popular were the Haughton School in St Saviourgate and Bedern School.

Haughton School

Haughton School was founded in 1770 by the benefactor William Haughton, a York citizen, who died at Coldbaths Fields in Middlesex three years later, and was brought back to be buried in Minster Yard in 1773.

He invested a considerable sum of money for the education of twenty boys of the parish of St Crux, providing places for boarders and day pupils, and the school was divided into preparatory, junior and senior. There were many governors including the Mayor, the Recorder, the Rector and Churchwardens of St Crux, and the overseers of the parish. The School was run by Mr G H Golledge for many years and old pupils were invited to join the Old Haughtonian's Association. The school was housed at 31 St Saviourgate, a three storey building with five bays at the front, built in 1735, and extended in 1739 (a rainwater head above marks this date).

Haughton School advertisment, York City Yearbook, 1921

Mrs Rene Sheard, whose father ran the Woolpack Inn on Peasholme Green, attended Haughton School, and her education was paid for by rather unconventional means,

And we had a good school master - Mr Golledge. My education was paid for by my schoolmaster's scotch whisky and Guinness. He used to come in.... at dinnertime, when school was empty, stand against the bar - his usual order a double whisky and a bottle of Guinness - and that was it - and my education was paid through that bill, no cash passed over. All the business people that had children, nearly all, went to Haughton School because it was so near. We had a good education, a marvellous education.

Mr Jack Birch, who lived next door to the school, remembers the whole family being taken there during the course of an air-raid in the First World War,

In June 1916 when I was just over five years old, I remember being woken in the night and being taken downstairs and we were taken, the whole family, into the next-door property which was Haughton School, run by a Dr Golledge. We finished up in the basement. Incidentally, there were no sirens. But the indication of an air-raid was that the electricity was turned very low, then came up again, and then it was turned out. It was possible to do this because the power station in Foss Islands Road generated direct current. What I remembered was, that to me, the basement or cellar, seemed quite a sizeable place; it's probably in fact very tiny. But Dr Golledge, very hospitable gentleman, produced baked potatoes in the middle of the night and that really stuck in my mind.

Mrs Law who lived in the shop opposite, in the 1940s, delivered groceries to the school,

It was dark and dingy in there with lots of panels in the hallway. It had a staircase going up and there was a lovely big balcony. Later on, children used to go there to sit for piano exams. A girl who came to see me said there was a great big skull on top of the stairs. The first exam she sat, she failed, and her mother was convinced it was because of this skull that frightened her.

Mr Cave recalls a tragic incident during the First World War connected with the Haughton School,

I remember Zeppelins coming over, passed over back of houses in St Saviourgate. There was a couple stood in the doorway, one was a soldier, and his young lady, at the end of St Saviourgate, and the bomb dropped and blew her foot off. And the foot landed through the Haughton school window and our headmaster actually picked [it up].

He also remembers,

You started school at four to fourteen, at least thirty in a class. We started nine to twelve, then two to four. Kids came from villages, a lot from Dunnington, Osbaldwick, Sheriff Hutton. These boarded. Every Friday morning they used to read us one of the Sherlock Holmes stories.

Bedern School

Most of the local children went to Bedern School, on the corner of Bedern and St Andrewgate, though conditions were not particularly good. Like most schools in the Victorian period and early part of the 20th century, discipline was strong and children feared their teachers. Bedern had the added 'delight' of its unpleasant environment, not just being situated in a poor, overcrowded area, but very close to the slaughterhouses, whose aroma even invaded the classrooms! Mrs Kay talks about her time there,

I started school when I was three years old. I'd be about five years old when we started lessons. It was, to my way of thinking, a very nice school. There was only one teacher I didn't like because he used to give us the cane. If you was even caught whispering, to the front and whack, the cane on the hand. Near school was a slaughterhouse, and we didn't like the animals being slaughtered.

We used to come out from school and they used to be swilling the streets after they'd slaughtered the animals. And that was in St Andrewgate - right opposite Bedern School.

We were taught just the fundamental things. We were taught to read, write, say the three R's, writing and arithmetic. We were taught the basics of learning how to keep house, sewing. We were taught to swim - but above everything we were taught to keep house. And from that school I went to St Denys School...in Piccadilly...which is now the TV studios.

Mr Chittock was another pupil of Bedern,

I remember playing truant with a man for three days off school, and me mother couldn't believe it when she took us to school and she found out we had. And the headmaster said, 'I'm going to give them a severe caning', and when we got home me mother asked us if he had, and I says, 'yes', and me mother gave us a good hiding as well.

Bedern School was a beautiful school as far as I'm concerned. We then went to St Denys School. That was the senior school. They wasn't interested in academic studies at all. Your mind was tuned more or less to sport. I used to swim for the school, play cricket, soccer and rugby. Used to go up to a place called Fenby Fields at Fulford, which was back of Lord and Lady Hatcherley's, right near St Oswald's Church.

The first electric lighting on the scene was when we went to Castlegate School and they used to sell scent cards, impregnated with scent, penny a piece to buy electricity for the school.

Mrs Greenley went to,

Bedern School when young. But when I was about eight, I left for Castlegate. Mother used to go into Bedern School and get me to go to the shops. 'Hurry up our May, and go to Wright's for a pork pie.' Took a jug and got a drop of gravy. Different at Castlegate. I got the cane once as I put a worm in teacher's inkpot and the teacher's daughter sat next to me and told. I won a prize for Brooke Bond writing competition for schools in York.

At Bedern it was there we signed the pledge, aged eight or nine, and anyone who signed the pledge got a free holiday. I went on the stagecoach to a woman called Mrs Bunney near Brandsby for a week. It was awful, I'd rather have been at home. And I've kept it (pledge). Never drink now except a sip at weddings.

Castlegate School

Mrs Cook,

went to Castlegate School. If you got the cane you never went home and told anyone. You might have got another. Teacher's word was law and your parents' was too. The teachers were old, had silvery hair. I remember reciting times table.

Mrs Dorothy Cook, 1995

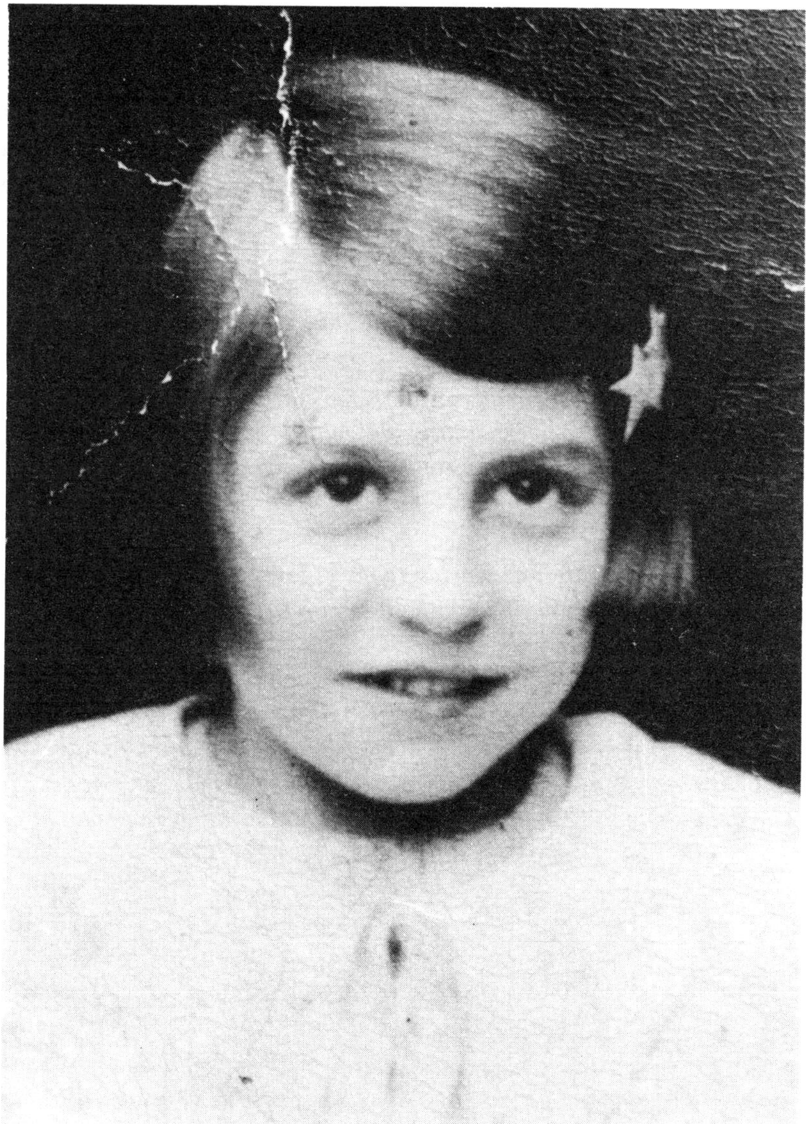

Dorothy Barker, Castlegate School, 1930

Mr Thompson also,

went to Castlegate School. Between Piccadilly and Fossgate is Merchantgate. Some steps went down and that was the playground. They tell me there is a tree planted somewhere there from the old scholars of Castlegate School. I went from there to Bedern School, then I went to the Model School, used to have to go to school on Saturday morning and have Wednesday afternoon off, the only school in York that did that. We was segregated. They had an A side and a B side, the good ones was on the A side.

Mrs Aldrich was another pupil of Castlegate,

A good school as well...in them days it didn't occur to you to answer anybody back. But one or two got cane. Just for simple things really...the headmaster was a Tartar, his word was it. There was one or two that was a bit cheeky, they just got a tap with a ruler on the knuckles. I remember writing on slates.

We were all assembled into this one big room and we marched to a hymn, the one prime minister Winston Churchill always liked.

I left there when I was twelve 'cos I won a scholarship to go to Queen Anne's. But me mother and father wouldn't let me go there 'cos they couldn't afford the books, so I had to carry on there and I'd lost an eye then and they said it would be too much strain on one eye, which was silly really. I could have gone. I'd no money to go with, but you had to buy your own uniform then and pay for your books. Well they just couldn't afford it.

We had a good time at school. We used to do exercises in the school ground. It was very cold...a big thick woolly scarf around you, fastened with a safety-pin again, no gloves on.

We had all the lessons in one day, every day. We started off with scripture, reading, spelling and then geography. Then we got on to sewing or the boys did handicraft work.

Mrs Butterworth also went to Castlegate :

When I went there, there was infants and they were mixed, but as you got older and you went upstairs, they were all girls, but I think that became to be mixed.

We used to have a little garden, and Craven's sweet shop, factory was there, at side of it.

We had a headmistress lived facing the church. A Miss Sylvester. She was strict. But there wasn't a lot of caning went on, because they were that strict with you, you had to do as you were told.

Mr Squire enjoyed his time there,

Teachers were marvellous. Miss Sylvester was headmistress. Then I went to the Model, they were too handy with the cane. If your clothes weren't up to their standard, you got the stick.

I went to Park Grove. Everybody in the class had to read, had to do joined up writing. I once got the stick because I didn't like Wordsworth, I objected to reading about daffodils.

Mr Birch actually walked out of the city centre to get to school,

I went to the primary at Fishergate, and we used to play in the yards, carefully segregated because the boys were in the right-hand yard and the girls in the left-hand yard, behind the school; and I can remember how all the lads used to play with cigarette cards, accumulating vast quantities of these, and sometimes using them as barter. They might even barter a pack of cigarette cards for tuppence or threepence, which could then be spent on sweets. But I do remember the time when mother had given me an apple which I had in the playground and I'd just finished eating this when one of the lads came up and said, 'Give us your core!' Would I give him what was left at the centre of the apple - which I did. I remember the teacher coming in to the playground and calling all the lads up to listen to some announcement which was on November 11th to announce that the war was over. I don't think that any of us really had an inkling what a tremendous occasion it was, but one of the staff, a young lady, just broke down in tears and rushed back into the school and we knew that it was serious. She probably had lost her fiance in the fighting.

Blue Coat School

A completely different establishment was the Blue Coat School, which was founded in 1705 for 40 poor boys to be "lodged, clothed, fed and taught". The same year, the Grey Coat School opened in Marygate for 20 poor girls. By 1818 the boys' school had increased their numbers to 52. No-one under eight or over ten was admitted except in special cases. Boys were bound apprentices under the direction of the Committee to learn husbandry, manufacturing or trade, some even being prepared for the Royal Navy, and if they were not successful in these areas, there was still the possibility of being put out to service in respectable families. Girls were placed in household service under the regulations of the Ladies' Committee. Both schools continued right up until 1946 when they became orphanages. Many York citizens were educated at the Blue Coat School including at least two Lord Mayors, Rhodes Brown, founder of W P Brown's department store, and Mr W H Thompson. When the latter was sworn in as Mayor in November 1943, the boys of the school formed a guard of honour.

Mr Ernest Webster was a pupil at the Blue Coat,

Oh, it was quite pleasant. We had school in morning and afternoon, just as I imagine the schools in York. But it was separated from them altogether. It was a school by itself... Very strict. You had to do as you were told. For a start off there was particular times for everything you had to do, like getting up in a morning. See, you had your own school to clean between you. The boys did their own dormitories out, swept and cleaned once a week. You weren't allowed out at all. Only with a teacher, or there was the eldest boy, took charge.

It was a big school, a big playing area. It was quite a nice place, though I can't say I liked it very much. You see the discipline was too much. Elmpark Way used to be a Blue Coat School cricket ground. Now in the corner used to be Amos's cottage and he was an ex-Blue Coat boy.

I remember the R101. We all went outside in the school yard to see it. Blotted out the whole sky. Somewhere near dinnertime it came over. It was a sight to see. Never seen an aeroplane.

Five o'clock was the getting up time, but everyone had to be out of the bedrooms by six..and all the beds had to be made up, and the dormitories left clean before they ever attempted to come out of them...We went to church every Sunday, twice, morning and afternoon...to St Michael's.

You'd no fires. Everybody had to go into the day room at seven o'clock. They had to be there, dressed, washed and everything. They'd see you'd cleaned your boots, polished 'em. They were given a good inspection. Yes, there was nobody in that school that went out dirty, I can tell you that now. The meals weren't bad. You were never hungry. When you finished your meal, you'd had sufficient.

Mr Webster's daughter admired the other skills that he had learned at the school, such as cooking and sewing, skills that boys did not usually learn elsewhere, and the sense of independence it brought,

It was a good upbringing. I'll give you an instance. My dad can sew, iron, cook. When I mean sew, I don't mean on a sewing machine. He can actually get the whole thing out.

Leatherwork, craftwork, woodwork, metalwork. You name it, they did it. If they wanted anything repairing, they did it themselves. If a chair broke they'd mend it.

But Mr Webster also explains that many boys were unhappy there, even though they probably had more food and better clothes than others in the Hungate area,

Ernest Webster, 1995

I ran away three times. Well I got a good thrashing when I got back. They caught me somewhere near Doncaster. As a youngster you never think. Get away from t'school as fast as you could. I'm afraid I was the ringleader. I took ten boys with me, but we weren't out long, I can tell you.

The only thing is, if I'd known then what I know now, I'd have been straight to the authorities. Me back was absolutely red raw. Oh, I'll never forget that thrashing. I'll never forget the feller that did it either. He never came anywhere near me when I was grown up. I never saw him. I would have belted him if I had. I don't know what my back must have been like, stripped down, your shirt off and hitting me with a cane. I'll never forget it.

You couldn't go to your parents or anything, unlike the kids at Bedern School. They got good thrashings there as well, but they went straight home and either the parents agreed with the teacher and gave 'em another one for being naughty, or their dad would be straight up to Bedern School and knock the living daylights out of the teacher. But you couldn't turn to anybody.

Yet despite this dreadful treatment, the strict discipline and stigma of being known as an orphan, he concedes that the regime did equip boys for the harsh world outside,

It was a tough school was that. You knew you'd been to school. The other kids what we call out of school, they didn't know a thing. You was taught, really taught, no doubt about that. Because we used to have 'em after tea. Well nobody in York schools had lessons after tea.

But they found us a job. You had a trade really when you left school. You could go anywhere. In fact a lot of the people in York that had workshops, used to try and get you on their list, for to go and work for them. We did everything you see, everything.

10, 11, 12 Drummond's Court and WCs at rear of 31 Hungate, 1930s

4

Industry and the Workplace

Like every other part of York, the parish of St Saviour had its share of men who were out of work. But the relatively small area was a rich source of employment, and the location of several major industries, such as the Flour Mill, the leatherworks, William Bellerby's Saw Mills in Hungate, the slaughterhouses and the Gas Company. There were also plenty of other smaller employers such as corn and hay merchants, iron founders, scrap merchants, coal merchants, undertakers (often combined with joiners), a brewery (John Hunt's, later the Ebor in Aldwark), salt merchants, chicory works, and laundries. Some people in the area were also self-employed tradesmen.

Bellerby's Saw Mills, now Derwent Coachworks, 1995

Leetham's Mill

The Flour Mill in Hungate had been founded by Henry Leetham in 1860. The premises were extended down to the Foss in 1885 and after Castle Mills lock was rebuilt in 1888, the mill was one of the main users of river traffic. Henry died in 1896, and a large number came to pay their respects at his funeral. His several sons and their families were able to carry on the business. In 1906 grain silos were constructed and then in 1909 further land was bought from the Corporation, but in 1911 the first strike took place at the mill. In 1916 the newspapers reported that the company had, in their service, the 'Anglia', the boat chartered to bring Cleopatra's Needle to England. Leetham's Mill was purchased by Spillers in 1928, closed in 1930 and the chimney demolished in January 1933. There is a large grave for twelve members of the Leetham family in York cemetery, with an ornate monument which has four angels on the corners. After 1937 the mill was used as a store for Rowntrees, but today it has become residential flats.

As a young boy, Andy Waudby would watch the workers at the mill,

The windows were sort of high up. Why, I don't know. P'raps because of the flooding. But then you had the opening to the mill and that's where we used to stand, watch the blokes in trousers and vest. Twelve hour shifts, lifting big bags o'flour. And then you had barges come up the river. A lot of people worked there, depending on the mill for a living. But if you'd seen those men, with just their trousers and vest, humping great big bags of flour - it wasn't work it was bloody slavery.

Mrs Butterworth's father,

worked at the flour mills, and we used to go down for our flour. We used to get it cheaper. A lot of Layerthorpe people worked there.

Reg Deighton's father felt he was fortunate to keep a job during the depression period,

He used to be a miller at Leetham's Mill in Hungate and when the mill burned down - I had five brothers and they was all working and he was offered a job in Southampton, which he surrendered to keep the five jobs in York, 'cos in the 1930s it was more important for everybody to be working, than one working and five not. So we stayed in York and my dad got a job at the gas company. He used to work for a Mr Blower.

Leetham's...had two fires, I understand, a small fire, then later on they had a large fire. But not long after, there was an argument about wages. They wanted to give 'em ten shillings a week less than what they was already being paid, and they was organising unions in those days. And they was the first to strike, and what they struck about was Leetham's.

It was certainly dangerous work. Mr Chittock's elder brother lost part of his thumb at the mill, and Mrs Thompson's father lost his finger there. But her grandfather had spent much of his life in the place,

It had a big chimley. My Granny and Grandad lived in Dundas Street and when they pulled the chimley down, he was in bed, very ill at the time, and he got up out of bed and stood at the window and watched them bring the chimley down. He was right upset, he cried his eyes out, 'cos he'd worked there nearly all the time at Leetham's mill until it closed down.

Jack Birch remembers,

that mill being burnt. The firm, round about here, constructed about 1933, the first part of what was being built for William Dove's in Piccadilly. I remember being on the top floor of that, when we were just topping out, when Leetham's Mill went up in flames. Tremendous conflagration.

I think the silos had been formed with heavy timbers built in a squared shape with corners interlocking, and something started off a fire, which went up these silos, and of course there was an awful lot of wood to burn, and it was a tremendous blaze.

Leetham's Mill, 1995

The Gas Works

Another major employer was the gas works. Gas had first come to York in 1824, after Royal Assent was given the previous year. Initially there were two companies, the York Union Gas Light Company and the York Gas Light Company, but these were amalgamated in 1844 and the York Gas Company formed. By 1912 the area of supply extended to seven miles from Ouse Bridge, covering all the villages in the immediate vicinity. The works were situated on the site now occupied by Sainsburys on Foss Bank.

Mr Waudby worked there,

After the war I got a job there and I had to give it up. It's big metal boxes, and they make saccharine tablets out of it. It's in layers and the gas used to come in and they used to seal all these boxes up, and the gas comes in at one end and it goes through all this powder, and come out at the other side. It sort of purified it.

Every now and again, they had to open one of these big boxes up, opened these steel tops off and three or four of us had to go down this ladder into it, and you had a crane which overhang, and we used to shovel this, and you had to break it up because it had gone hard when the gas had gone through. While you were working down there the gas used to be leaking sometimes out of the next thing, so you felt dizzy or sick. You had to get out quick. I went poorly and the doctor told me I had to give it up because of the gas.

But carburettor water gas... it was a bit risky as well because when we weren't emptying the boxes, we used to make this gas and we used to put the coke up on a hopper of a crane, a hoist, pull these big things on wheels, they used to go up and they'd drop it into this fire and seal it. Well the bloke who operated it come off too fast with the wheel at top. Well, bang! The whole thing used to explode, whumph, it didn't half used to go off. If you was eating sandwiches, if you were on your shift, you were eating muck.

Then you had to get these steel bars, open these doors and at bottom of this big fire and put about five of these bars into the fire bars to hold all the fire up. Then we used to get a big hook with a big pole and rake inside and get the clinkers out, then at a given time you'd pull the bars out and let the fire drop down. It was hard work.

Mrs Butterworth remembers the works,

It was really interesting. They used to put whatever it was they burned to make the cinders in these big things and when they was ready for coming out they used to open it and there was a flame and there used to be a stream run down and they used to rake 'em out before they could come to be sold. Then there was Walkers coal yard on Layerthorpe Bridge. We had a pram and used to go to gas house for sixpennorth o' cinders, twice on Friday for two lots o' coal and two lots o' cinders, and they used to last all week.

A lump of coal, a couple of shovels of cinders, you'd a fire going all night in them grates. And we were always warm. You never seemed to feel the draughts in them houses.

It was half-a-crown for your coal and sixpence for your cinders. So for six shilling you'd a fire all week. And now I think it's about six pound a bag or something like that.

Reg Deighton was one of the many children who queued to get coke from the works,

Every Saturday morning - tanner's worth o' coke, and you used to sew two bags together, cos you got a bagful. It was no use going with a small bag. You went with the biggest bag you could possibly get.

Everybody had a barrer. Used to make one. Well we used to have the two wheels and it was good 'cos when it snowed you used to pull it, the wheels used to lock and it would act like a sledge. You just pulled the thing through.

But the smell was rather strong, and seemed to pervade the whole area, as Mr Deighton recalls,

It smelt of sulphur. You see coke, you throw cold water on it, it's like oxidey sulphury smell. Well what happened there - they used to push the coal into the ovens, then they used to push the coke out when they'd got all the gases and what have you out. The coke used to drop into like a conveyor belt that was running water. As soon as the coke dropped in there y'got that terrible smell come off it. But it was lovely and warm in there on a cold day, used to go in there and stand to get warm while you waited to get your coke. It used to be back of Hungate, the coking yard.

Mrs Fearn,

used to go there with barrers to get coke. Twice a week , sometimes in winter. If you had a younger brother or sister, you used to push them there in the barrer whilst it was empty and stick 'em on top of your cinders coming back. We always had a barrow. Out of an old pram. Get a box, two wheels, Bob's yer uncle.

And the men who used to fill 'em for us, they were ever so good. You used to take a bag sometimes, hold your bag open and they'd keep putting it in. And you went and asked for so much in measurement, and invariably before he closed that bag he'd dump you some more in.

For Ted Chittock, memories of the works are much less happy,

I belong to a family of eight. My father was scalded to death when I was four years of age, at the gas works. A lot of people worked at the gas works on Foss Islands, which is now Sainsburys store. He was scalded to death something like six months before the Workmen's Compensation Act came in. So as a result of that, my mother never got any compensation for eight children. So she went out and she sold the Yorkshire Evening Press from all that time ago in 1926 right up to the start of the Second World War and she used to stand on top of the gents' toilets in Parliament Street.

Mrs Chittock at a street party, Hungate, 1929

For women there were few alternatives. Domestic or factory work were often the only options. When she left school, Mrs Aldrich went to clean at a house in Blossom Street,

It was a big house and I got five shillings a week for that. But you was at it from morning 'til latish at night. But they were pretty good to me there and I always remember they gave me my dinner, but I had to have it in a room on my own - couldn't have it with them, weren't allowed that.

And then I went to Armstrong Oilers on Lendal Bridge and worked there. That was four and eleven a week...I got fed up of long hours. It was eight 'til five or six at night. Worked right through, just breaked to sit down for your dinner and that was it. We made oilers for trains, for the axle boxes. It was very dirty and heavy, often got cut with steel. A long length of steel on a machine; put it in a certain hole to get a bend on the end of it to a certain length. They was all riveted together, and then they were padded with wool and the feeders used to hang down.

Louisa Grant, at a Women's Land Army Reunion, 1949

Mrs Louisa Aldrich, 1995

Mrs Hall,

would have liked to have taken hairdressing up but in them days it was factory work. I left school at Christmas and started at Terrys. We had to go to Layerthorpe Bridge to catch a bus to Bishopthorpe factory. I think it was tuppence. We didn't get much in wages, it was eleven shillings and that was with a Saturday morning as well.

Mr Deighton lived next door to Clancy's rag and bone merchants in St Andrewgate,

Mrs Clancy was a rather large woman who used to sit in the office and pay you for the rags and rabbit skins that you used to take in. Jim, her husband, used to do all the hard work, hanging the rabbit skins, and sorting the rags and the iron from the brass and the copper. And he used to do all the loading of the wagons and things. But she used to just sit in the office and pay the money. And twice a week one of the jobs I used to do for Mrs Clancy, I used to get a penny, was to go to Davy Hall in Davygate and buy a jug of soup with a dumpling in it, and that used to be their lunch.

Mrs Kay remembers Clancy's,

The only time we ever went was when they started pulling the houses down. And us kids what was left we used to get buckets or any old container and go round the old rubble and pick up any old piece of iron we could find, nails, anything that Clancy's would take, and we used to get money for it.

Slaughterhouses

Another main source of employment in the area was rather more unpleasant, with even more dreadful smells than the gas works. Reg Deighton describes the slaughterhouses,

At the back of the house there used to be Pump Yard, where there was three slaughterhouses, where cattle was slaughtered and taken into York Market on a Saturday to be sold.

The worst smells used to come from the slaughterhouses, which was out and about and all over the place. Bowman's used to slaughter at the end of Bedern. And then Wright's pork butchers used to slaughter in Aldwark. But in St Andrewgate up Pump Yard, there used to be two or three slaughterhouses up there. It used to smell awful, specially when they was boiling the pigs. They used to kill the pigs and then boil 'em to scrape all the bristle off 'em. And it was a smell I never used to like.

After market day they all used to be driven through the streets. There was no carts or anything like that to deliver 'em. Now the worst thing I can remember about that was the back of the Shambles, where Newgate Market is now. That used to be a big corral for the cattle. All the slaughterers in t'Shambles, about five or six used to slaughter the cattle themselves, using the same slaughterhouse, in many cases, but different butchers. And they used to drive the cattle up and into the Shambles into this big compound sort of style, and they used to turn them loose in there and when they wanted them they'd all be branded with their particular mark. They used to go and catch 'em and pull 'em into the slaughterhouses and kill 'em. And there was no humane killer - it used to be pole-axe. Just pull 'em down and hit 'em with a long spike into the head. That killed them. It wasn't a thing I'd really go and sit and watch. We'd go and sit and watch the cattle coming, but I never really enjoyed watching 'em - slaughterers. I don't think I could have become a butcher meself.

I remember the foul smell was the skin yard just inside Layerthorpe, where they used to take sheepskins and they used to cure them. Used to put 'em in lime, in pits. It all used to go into the Foss this stuff when they'd finished with it, they'd empty the vats and tanks and what have you - straight into the Foss. And down into the Ouse.

Andy Waudby actually worked in a slaughterhouse when he was fourteen,

It was real hard work. It was Bowman's butchers in Goodramgate. Nowadays they make sausage skins out of plastic, but in those days you had sausage skins made out of sheep's guts. When they'd killed a sheep, I used to pull the skin through and then I had to wash it, and it would be put in a basket, and it used to go to the sausage skin maker. And there they used to scrape 'em. They'd get the gut, and it used to be a sausage machine and used to stuff all meat in and stuff were in there, bread and what-have-you.

I had to deliver the meat on a Saturday morning in a big carrier bike. I used to push this heavy bike all round Heworth with the meat in and one old lady, every Saturday morning used to give me my breakfast, egg and some bacon, and I used to get a bit of breakfast for nowt.

When Wally Holmes was about nine or ten, he helped out at the slaughterhouse,

In summertime, holiday time, you'd go to cattle market on a Monday. Butchers used to buy their beasts and one thing and another. Well just down Walmgate on left hand side, where INL Club is today, was all slaughterhouses. Well we used to go round there, and help 'em wi' ropes to pull bullocks in and they used to have what they called a bell humane killer. Held it on to bullock's head and then banged the end of it.

Mrs Fearn played near the slaughterhouses,

There was two slaughtering days a week. And we used to go down, and the girls were worse than the boys, and we used to sit on the wall, and they used to know we were out there, did the slaughterers, and the offal never went into the shops. It used to come out to us. The liver, the kidneys; and the lights as they call 'em, used to go to the cats. And we used to get all the offal. We used to go wi' your little bag, and I've seen us sit there on slaughtering day, and we used to take some paper with us to wrap our stuff in. And we used to sit on this wall and we used to make boats of paper and there was the guttering where they used to let all this blood and everything run out, and we used to float our paper boats in blood in t'guttering. See which would go fastest. Red sails in the sunset.

Mrs Sheard,

had a slaughterhouse in Black Swan yard, and I can remember now standing watching 'em bleeding the pigs, 'cos they used to strap 'em down to bleed them. Me mam had a pet pig, Bet, which never left the back door.

In 1935 the Council made a new byelaw about slaughterhouses, repealing the previous byelaws of 1890, which required the owners to have licences, and brought in much tighter restrictions. These included the use of the correct receptacles, which must be cleansed thoroughly and their contents removed every twenty-four hours. There had to be adequate ventilation and drainage, the whole area should be cleansed within three hours of each slaughter, no pets were allowed on the premises, and above all, there should be plenty of fresh water available. These simple steps had never before been enforceable!

There were other small employers in the area, and Mr Deighton remembers living close to Rymer's undertakers at 35 St Andrewgate,

I can remember running errands for Jack Rymer's mother. She was a big woman, with a large chest, and I was a little lad and she used to come about three doors up and I used to look up and I could never see her face - because I was so small and looked up and everything was uplifted.

Jack Rymer had a big shop at the back. It was a wooden building, used to see all his tools, that he made his coffins. It was a marvellous workshop to go into.

And Mrs Sheard remembers,

There was a little building which was the Haymarket. Do you know the great big iron weight - that's why they call it the hay weight, where the farmers used to weigh all their hay. I don't remember seeing farmers with loads of hay, but this little railing, there was a man in there of course, checking.

Mr Hall was employed further away,

I went apprentice blacksmith at Wedgewoods on Holgate Road. It was six shillings a week and I had to be there at 6.30 in the morning to get the fires going, and I left at 5.30 at night. Such a lot of horses about, there was Wickham's and Frank Green's on the Mount, they had hunters. Colonel Kirby's at Poppleton Road and Rutherford's coal people in Rougier Street. Great big heavy cart-horses. I was like a pea on a drum on top of one of them. Where Lil lived there was Bellerby's joiners. They had a big black horse and they said, 'When t'lad goes home, let him bring it back'. I put some string round its bit and got up on its back and riding it down, got over Ouse Bridge and a tram came by and it nearly had me off. Got to the top of Hungate with me, well there was some devils of kids there and they shouted things and it started galloping down Hungate with me and round the corner to the stable. Chap there said it hadn't been out o't stable for a fortnight. No wonder!

And Mr Thompson walked from Hungate to Rowntrees every day,

I worked at Rowntrees for 49 years. They could give you two hours' notice. I was lucky. They could sack you when you was 18, then war came so they kept us on. We got called up for the forces and when we came back they had to keep your job, and that service counted. After two years they started putting you on the staff, so I'd had five years.

In the late 19th and early 20th century, chicory manufacturing became popular in York. The crop was actually grown outside the city, in Dunnington. One of the first York merchants was Henry Wilberforce, father of William, who operated in Walmgate. Thomas Smith occupied premises on Lower Orchard Street and Foss Bank.

Mr Deighton remembers,

The other place that used to smell, on the front of Foss Bank there was Chicory Yard - and they used to get this chicory smell coming out of it, which used to be added to Lyons Coffee. The liquid coffees that you could buy in those days. Coffee and chicory used to be mixed to make a modern drink. And that used to smell terrible.

Laundries

Something of a contrast to the vile-smelling industries, were two laundries, the York Sanitary Steam Laundry (formerly Yorkshire Laundries Ltd) just past the Black Swan on Peasholme Green, and York County Hygienic Laundry, round the corner on Foss Islands. In 1930, there were six other laundries in York as well as six Chinese laundries.

Mrs Greenley's mother,

was head laundress on Peasholme Green, when young, really good at ironing and crimping. She did doctor's shirts for threepence each to wash and iron. They came round with six at a time.

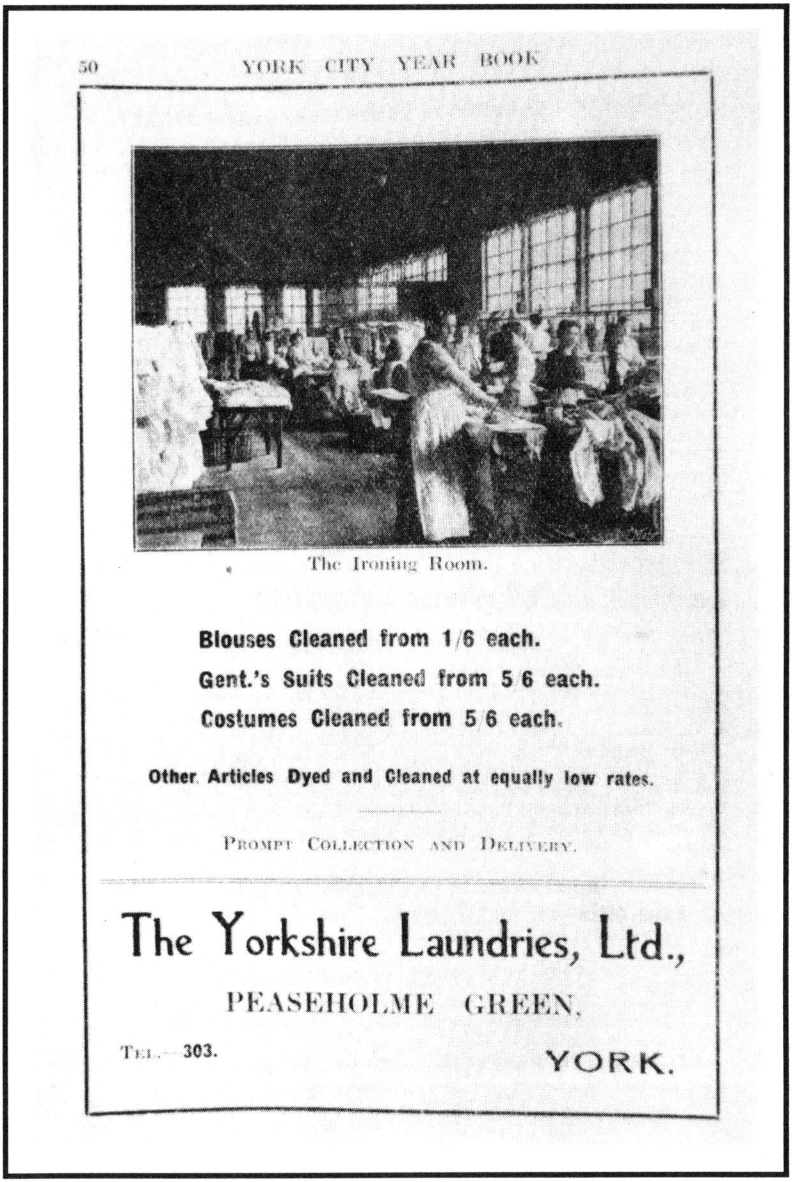

Yorkshire Laundries Ltd, Peasholme Green, York City Yearbook, 1920

Mr Waudby's mother worked at the laundry,

She was one of the finest in York for steam, she was very clever at it. The Hygienic was owned by Mr Clark. It employed a good few women and I went there for a while. I was a van lad. Remember Dad's Army, well you know the old man - Jones's van - well Hygienic had a couple of those.

I used to go with John Stringer to Scarborough, to the big hotels to get laundry. John used to wear breeches and leggings. John and me were coming back from Scarborough; we got to the top of Whitwell Hill, the van went out of control in the frost, and we went round and round like that down Whitwell Hill and finished up in the middle section. It wasn't half hair-raising.

Ted Chittock worked at the York Sanitary Laundry,

I left school in July 1936. Went to Rowntrees and invariably, from the very offset, you was on short time. You'd go in the morning, go back to work at the afternoon, card wasn't there, you was on short time. Consequently come Christmas time there was a lot of us sacked. We went from there to what was the York Sanitary Laundry in Peasholme Green. I went to work as a van boy. Me wage was eight and fourpence a week and I worked from eight o'clock in a morning 'til about nine o'clock at night, and one half day was on a Wednesday, when I finished at four o'clock at night, for me half day. Now eight and fourpence is less than fifty pence in today's money.

Some men were self-employed, and had to be innovative, finding ways to make a living. Mrs Sheard's father, Fred Wright, was advised to leave the Woolpack Inn and go into business on his own in the haulage trade. She tells the story,

He didn't start up in the haulage business 'til quite late - sort of semi-retired, and went to number one Haymarket. And we lived exactly next door to an old chap, he was a cabbie, and he used to do funerals. And I can always remember that the seat that he sat on was all glass underneath it, and little babies' coffins were in that little glass seat underneath.

Me dad used to do a lot of haulage for Birch's, help 'em out when they were busy, with him having wagons. He had sixteen horses at one time, horses and carts. And it was a sight for sore eyes to see them all turn out to go to the Stray for the evening. That was their walk, when the lads had finished their work. Many a time I used to go with them on the horses' backs.

Me dad was a bit of a lad. He used to go to a lot of farmers, and I remember sitting round the farmer's table with all the farm lads, the farmer there with the joint of beef, and he used to be sharing the meat out on the plates, used to say, 'What about bairn, Fred? Does she like a bit o' fat with her meat?' I used to go around all the farms, come back loaded with apples and stuff, and we had a...trap. Horse and trap. And we had this special horse called Dick, and it was really a hunting horse. Dad used to go to the country a lot, have one or two too many, fall asleep in the trap and Dick used to bring him home, just tip the trap up, tip dad out.

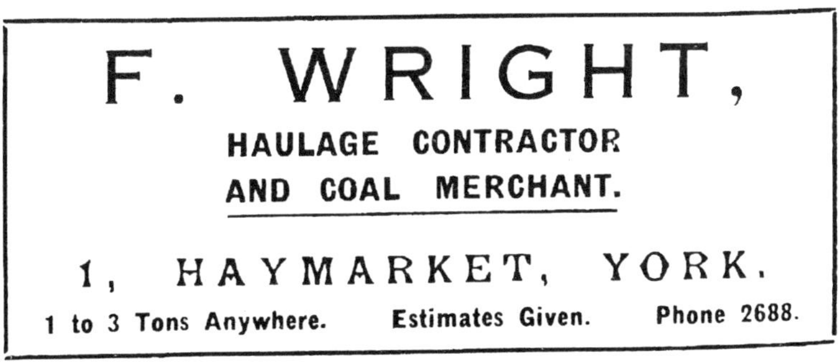

Fred Wright, Haulage Contractor, Haymarket, 1930

Mr King-Reynolds remembers his father renting out stables to Fred Wright (Mrs Sheard's father),

There was always the lovely smell of horses at the bottom of the garden. My brother and I used to go and stand at the bottom of the garden as lads and it always had an air of mystery. In the very old days Grandfather Reynolds had horses and his wife used to ride and he himself had a pony and trap for going round and visiting his patients.

Mr Squire's father,

was in the 8th Hussars in the First World War and by trade he was a saddler. He used to sell fish, got a horse and cart and went round villages, a barrel of herrings to Dunnington, Warthill, Stockton-on-Forest. I could have all the fish I wanted. I've eaten herring six days a week. My mother used to pickle them, 24 in a tray. Then second hand furniture, he could do it up because he was a saddler.

When Andy Waudby was ten, he used a barrow to do errands,

If you knew somebody who worked at railway they had iron wheeled carts, and somebody could get firewood or stuff cheap, so you got iron wheels like that. You go to Melia's or Meadow Dairies, they would give you a big Danish Bacon box, about four foot, and about three foot wide. Strong thick wood. You had to set off and put wheels on these boxes. A barrer was a thing that could save you money and get you things. Come Saturday, 'Do you think you could go to gasworks and get us some coke?' And she'd gi' us threepence. Up Hungate, you'd see all the little lads wi' the barrers. Every Saturday morning. And for an extra tuppence, you'd get a bag on top o' that. Now by that time it were bloody heavy. Now you're talking about us at ten years old. We pulled those barrers all the way back to Hungate. We could make about sixpence on a Saturday morning. Then you'd get somebody as wanted some logs somewhere. So we'd walk right up to top of Layerthorpe for somebody to get a barrowload.

By the time he was fourteen, he had a carrier-bike,

delivering fruit and vegetables. I also did cleaning and scrubbing floors for 12 shillings a week. I would cycle until 9.30 at night after starting at 8 am.

After that he worked at a place called Mooney's,

I remember being on a machine cutting steel. I was sat there and the machine going up and down. There was this steel rolling out, and I was whistling away, not saying a word to nobody, happy with the world and I got such a ruddy bat. 'Gerron with your work, stop whistling, your mind in't on job.' I worked on a circular saw at fifteen. And this was teak, heavy teak wood. There was a big saw there and a littler, smaller blade. Used to get these big pieces of teak, I was only fifteen years old don't forget, this great big saw going round, and we used to push this wood through the saw and it used to slice the wood 'til it was about that thick. Then it went upstairs to some women who were sat at drills and they were like little washers, and these were made for Armstrong Oilers.

I used to cut out these pieces of wood, so these women could make buttons. Now these women, there'd be about six of 'em, and they were on piece work. Now you know a tea chest, I had to fill one of those boxes, wi' slices of wood like that, right to top, before I got two shilling. So I had to go like the bloody clappers to fill one before I got two bob.

During the depression, men were laid off and unemployment increased. The Means Test meant that people did not receive any more than the very minimum to keep alive. And when, in winter, there was the opportunity of a few hours' work shovelling snow, the competition was fierce, as Mr Waudby explains,

Poor fellers, they used to run like hell, as fast as they could go to Foss Islands to get a job. To earn summat. Don't get the idea the people were lazy. They weren't given the chance to work. There was no work, and they had this Means Test. And if a young lass got a job at Rowntrees, the mother, the father was kicked off the dole straight away. And the daughter's money had to keep 'em.

The Yorkshire Evening Press of 16th January 1933 reported a snowfall of three inches, which was received with joy in some quarters,

Although to some the outlook was dismal ... to the unemployed it was quite a welcome sight. The staff at the Employment Exchange were at the offices in Parliament Street before six o'clock. At this hour there were ten men outside and others soon began to collect ... orders came intermittently up to 8.15. Altogether 207 unemployed men were engaged, and the footpaths and streets were cleared of snow by the afternoon.

5

A Wealth of Shops

There were many corner shops in the area, and the community could get most of what they wanted locally, without the need to venture further into the town centre. There were also plenty of tradesmen who came round the streets selling their wares.

Mr Holmes remembers some of these characters,

Mr Squires, the potman, used to come round Hungate hawking his pots with his horse and cart. Then Machin he used to come round...selling all odds n'sods off his hand cart. Sometimes fish, sometimes brooms, sometimes mushy peas - a right mixture. Machins were a well known Hungate family.

Then there's Mrs Sampson, the ginger pop lady who used to sit at end of Wide Yard in Hungate. She'd sit out there with her case full of ginger beer which we used to buy, then we broke the top off the bottle to get at the glass marble. We'd go playing marbles then with the glass stopper tops.

Mr Moore the milkman had a little shop near the end of Aldwark and he used to come round with his milk there with his pony and cart. The shops...were very small and they had Cadbury's chocolate on the glass, you see the same when you go to the Castle Museum. Could get toffees and lollipops and toffee apples.

Mrs Kay recalls,

Pearson's was our milkman, and he used to come round every day with an urn, one that you could carry. And if you heard him coming, you went to wait at the door with your jug, and he used to ladle half a pint out, or a pint, whichever you needed. No pasteurised, no sterilised, straight from the cow.

They used to come round with their little carts and horses, and Rag n'Bone...if you gave 'em anything - kids got a balloon.

Mrs Fearn remembers another familiar name,

There was Kipper Jack, I think he was a mute. He used to trot along and he had this big basket, all spotlessly clean, always a teacloth on it, and he used to have muffins in it.

The corner shops usually had signs on the walls outside, advertising various items, such as Lyons Tea, Lyons Cakes, Borwicks Baking Powder, Rinso, Min Cream cleans better, Colmans Wash Blue for snow white linen, and Wild Woodbines.

Andy Waudby would go into the corner shop,

and ask the old lady if she had any 'Wild Woodbines'. When she said 'yes', we would say, 'Well you want to tame them then.'

To children, the most important shops were the ones which sold sweets, and Ted Chittock was a regular visitor to Alf Huckle's shop, which displayed the familiar Lyons sign,

On the corner of Haymarket and Haver Lane. When we was children, we used to have a bill at Alf Huckle's shop. We could go in there and say, 'Could we have these sweets', and at the end of the week he was paid.

Mr Squire was not so lucky, he only remembers that Alf, "clouted kids for looking in the window."

According to Mrs Sheard,

On Haymarket there was a small sweetshop, and this chap used to loan cycles out for sixpence an hour, and I believe his name was Mr Moore. And he also had a little shop in St Saviour's Place near the Woolpack.

Alf Huckle's Shop and Haymarket Inn, 1930s

Mr Birch also liked his sweets,

I remember in George Street there was a very attractive sweetshop that sold gobstoppers. These were large round sugary sweets that took a long time to suck to nothing and therefore the high price, they were about a penny a piece, probably made quite a good profit for the shopkeepers because they were in constant demand.

Mrs Fearn would go to Annie Binns' shop on Dundas Street, which sold, "mostly sweets. Your eyes used to pop when you used to go in."

Of course, children often had to do the shopping for their parents and Mrs Kay would be sent to Wright's butchers,

I remember going for pigs' feet on a Thursday. And she'd send you with a basin and tuppence and you used to come out with red hot pig's feet with all the gravy dipping, they were beautiful. Now that was a meal for us, two pennorth, and that fed us all, with there being seven of us.

Mrs Butterworth also did the shopping,

You went to Comyn's for three pennorth of bacon pieces and a sixpenny shank. You knew who was good to you, you used to stand and wait for them. Used to go to Cross's bacon shop in Fossgate, but Tommy Cross had a butcher's shop in the Shambles.

Then Slater's for your flour and your yeast, can't beat your own baked bread. We used to go to Cross's, take a basin for a pound of black treacle and my mother used to bake all her own bread and we used to have hot treacle in cakes for tea, which was very nice. We used to take a basin and a jug to Scott's for their savoury ducks and a jug for gravy. As they came out of the oven they were all soft and then they'd put them in a basin for you, and what was left he used to make into cubes and sell them as penny ducks.

Mr Thompson remembers going out,

to the market looking for damaged goods. It was on until nine o'clock at night. They used to sell off cheaply 'cos there was no cold storage. We used to go to t'Shambles on Sunday morning shopping for cheap meat. And fish and chips, tuppence for fish and a pennorth of chips. Used to go to Scott's for penny ducks. Wright's butchers at top of Aldwark had 30 or 40 pigs hanging there. Go to Wright's on a Monday morning for pig's feet.

Mrs Aldrich was able to buy a lot for a penny in those days,

Sweets for a week. We got them from ... Sally Dixon's and there was another shop, we used to call him Greedy Amos. He was Greedy as well. At the bottom end of St Saviourgate there was Moore's. That was cakes, tea cakes, bread and milk. When the market was on, we'd go round and see if they'd left any orange boxes. We used to take them home for firewood, and see if there was any fruit they didn't want.

Mrs Felton would look forward to her older sister Rene (Mrs Thompson) to come in so that she would go to the shop for biscuits.

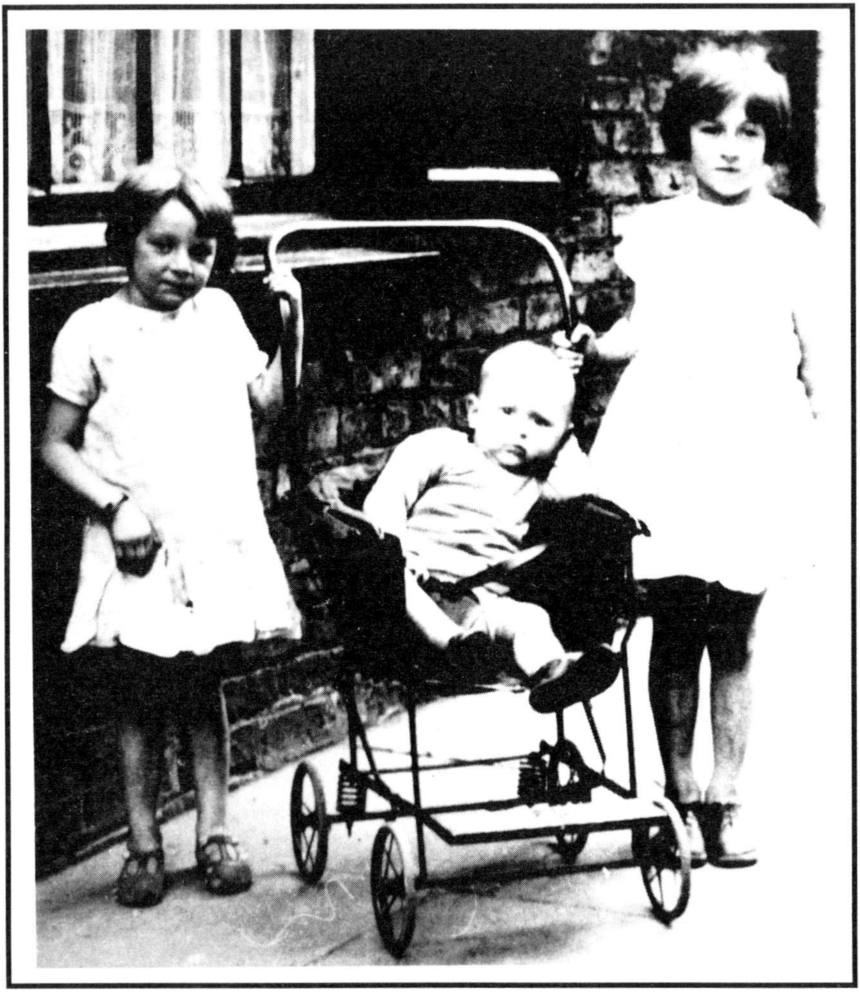

Irene and Cecelia Thorpe, Stonebow Lane, 1934

Mrs Irene Thompson (top) and Mrs Cecelia Felton, 1995

Mrs Thompson explains,

You used to go in with a penny and just ask for a pennyworth of broken biscuits, give you a bag full. And there was machines along on the corner, and cigarette machines as well. I used to go for my auntie's cigs in the machine. Craven A's she used to smoke.

As Mrs Felton describes,

They were in a little paper. They wasn't sealed up. Just in a little packet with five cigarettes in.

Ted Chittock remembers another shop in Hungate,

Wheatley's, the football player ... his mother owned a shop and it was amazing, where they were selling margarine and butter and alongside it was a can of paraffin. They pumped it out for lamps.

In Hungate was Dan's fish 'n chip shop. You could get one of each for tuppence or something like that. Next door to her there was Mrs Bardy, who made lemonade and toffee apples.

Valerie Shirbon lived with her mother and sister in a sweet shop at the corner of St Saviourgate, near Salem Chapel,

Our shop sold sweets, tobacco, groceries, tea and sugar, cough medicine, combs, bandages, a few dolls for presents, drinks, soap, ice-cream. Everything. The business failed when the supermarket was built called Carling's supermarket where the Halifax is. We bought goods there for Mum to sell in the shop, like six tins of peas as she couldn't afford 48 tins wholesale. It was a real good business in 1948 time. My sister and I helped as we got older. There was an old-fashioned till with a drawer, and sliding glass doors on the window. We had to make sure the glass doors were closed so people outside couldn't see us go into the till. Used to have fire in the fireplace, couldn't have it very hot because of the chocolate. Locals came in and workers from Spen Lane - Birch's, Rymer's, Heppell's joiners of Aldwark.

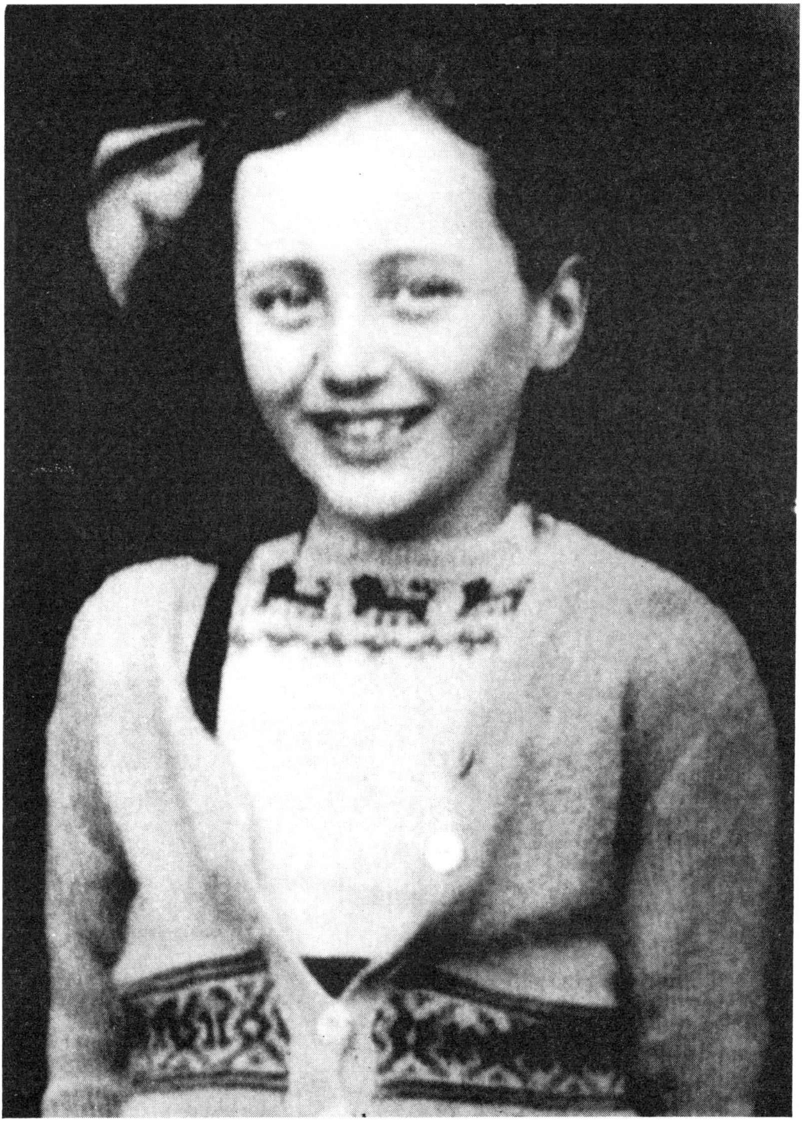

Valerie Shirbon, aged 10

If it was cold they came behind the counter to get warm. 'Where's the chair?' they'd say, we had a nice big chair. A customer could sit in it, came to sit and would chat for ages. Old fashioned brass scales, we used to clean. Sweets were stored on shelves all way round the room. We had glycerine and honey cough medicine, we called it 'icky picky wine'. If my sister and I had a cough, we would go and get a bottle of that wine.

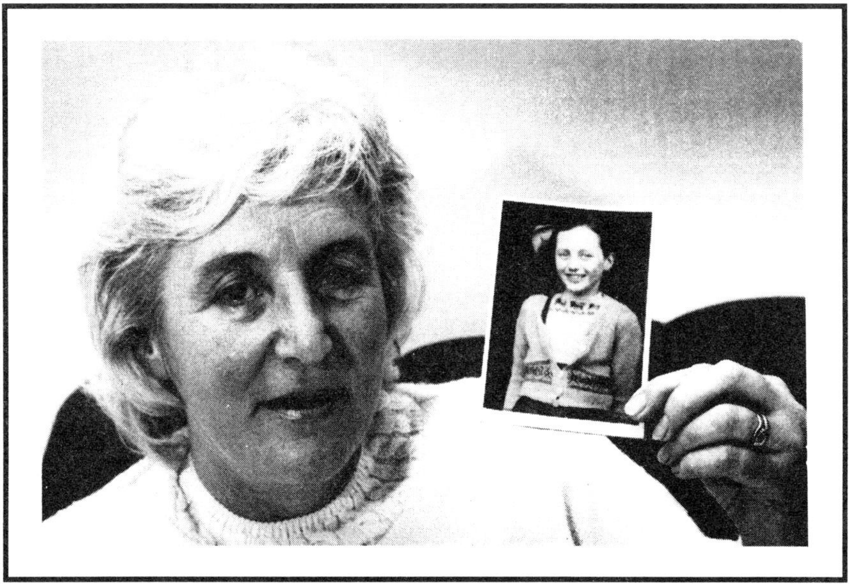

Mrs Valerie Law, 1995

Boys from Rowntrees, Forestry Commission and other companies came to Blue Coat School to do continuation classes and one boy pinched a whole jar of liquorice torpedoes. They used to come at a quarter past 10 as they had a fifteen minute break and one day she noticed there was a whole jar of liquorice torpedoes missing so she rang up. They went down to the classroom to ask them, and they all said 'no' but there was one boy missing. And he'd pinched it and then he didn't know what to do with it, so he ran to Layerthorpe Bridge and threw it in the river. But they made him pay.

One of the best remembered shops was Billy (Slasher) Calpin's barber shop, at the top of St Saviourgate. Mr Holmes recalls,

If you wanted a basin cut ... like a Mohican. Cut up both sides. Many used to go for a shave as well. There was a hell of a lot down Hungate, the families themselves would drop a basin on and cut round the edges. Then when you was going somewhere special, that was when you go up to hairdresser's.

Mrs Butterworth also knew Billy,

He was a Walmgate lad was Billy Calpin. But he was there years and years. It was nearly all men. My father used to go there, my husband used to go there, me brothers used to go. Billy used to charge 'em threepence for their haircuts.

Mrs Fearn was one of the few girls who had her hair cut there,

He was full cousin to me mother, and we never used to pay, he never took any money off us. Everybody went to him. If you wanted your beard trimming, anything, Billy would do it for you. It was a very small place, one room actually. There was these two steps, used to go up and they'd all be sat round this room, and he had a little room off it, where he used to have a sink to wash his hands. There's a programme on television, and it's in America and it just reminds me sometimes of that, where they all sit and talk - nobody goes in to get their hair cut. They used to go to put a bet on. And more or less sit just for company. It must have been a nice atmosphere for them. And how he made his living out of it, I don't know, but he did. And he liked a drop of the hard stuff did Uncle Billy.

Andy Waudby's grandfather had a fish shop at 11-12 Fossgate, with a very ornate frontage which can still be seen,

You've never seen owt like it in your life. It was a big fish-shop, all round was game hung up and there was water playing on to this big slab, all the time, and at the side you had poultry. Today if you look up you'll see the German eagle, it's still there, with my grandad's initials underneath it. And then you had the farmworkers. They would come in a bus on a Saturday.

Waudby's fish shop, now an Italian restaurant, Fossgate, 1995

Coppergate most all day long used to be loaded wi'farmers. And they'd stay there biggest part o't day while their wives were flogging cheese and butter. I always remember the butter all had lovely patterns on, in fact my granny used to love to go there and get eggs.

The German Eagle, Fossgate, dated 1898

Many people remember Rieveleys corn merchants, who had a warehouse, storing hay and straw, near St Saviour's Church. They also owned a pet shop just within Colliergate. Mrs Felton would look in the window,

A window full of little chickens. Little tiny yellow chickens. And there used to be this light in the middle where they used to all cuddle round.

Mrs Thompson would also go to the shop for seed for her Granny's bird,

They had loads of birds inside, and parrots and goldfish. There was a big macaw ... they used to have it outside on a stand.

Mr Burnett also went into Rieveleys,

When you went in the shop there was sacks of seed. Used to get stuff off floor and go out in streets trying to catch pigeons. Would ask for sixpennyworth of pigeon pie toffee, bloke would give you a bat across t'ear.

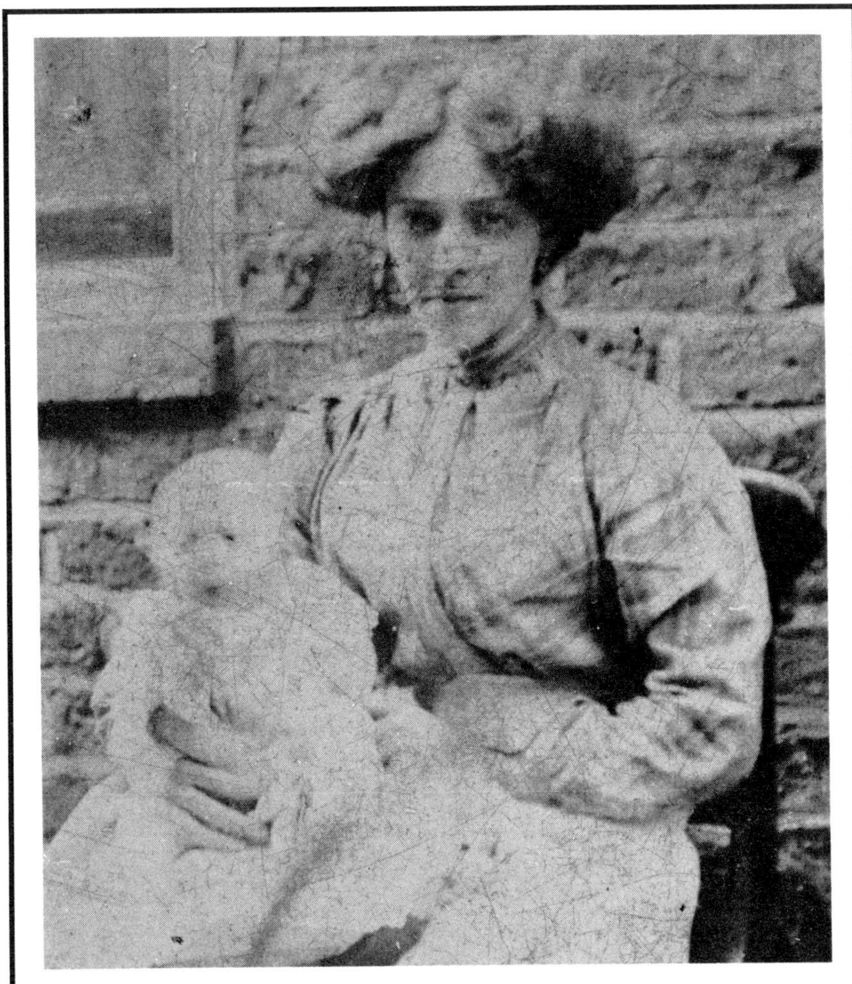

Harry Burnett and mother, 1920

Pawnbrokers

The other common type of shop in the area, which has disappeared today, was the pawnbroker. There were three local ones, as Wally Holmes remembers,

There were Merriman's, Hardcastle's and Sharpe's. Sharpe's was the nearest of the lot, on the corner of St Saviourgate and Colliergate. A big thing in those days was taking a suit down. Daddy's suit used to go in on Monday morning and then on Friday it'd come back out again.

Mr Squire was often sent to the pawnbrokers when he was a boy,

I took the eiderdown and Witney blankets to Merriman's and got ten shillings, then got told off for being late for school. I redeemed them for eleven shillings later in the week.

Mrs Sheard knew of people who tried to pawn clothes unsuccessfully,

Some of the stuff they refused to take because they used to take them in as husbands took things off, vests and things. 'Take it home first and wash it, then bring it back clean and then I can loan you'.

Mrs Butterworth's neighbour was a regular customer,

There was a woman who lived in the next yard to us, she used to take washing in and she used to wash it and pawn it, and she'd get it out again for people to come for it, and then she'd get paid. But me mam never pawned because we'd nothing to pawn. We were always tidy and we'd all be a little bit different for a Sunday from what we used to go to school in.

6

Leisure Time

Apart from the pubs and children's playgrounds, there was little in the way of entertainment, and no money for expensive pleasures. But in spite of this, people managed to find ways to enjoy themselves. There was sport, of course. The Woolpack had its own rugby team, and there was also boxing, practised at the Hungate Boys' Club. Those who could afford it would go to the cinema, and forget their worries by escaping into the latest dreams on offer from Hollywood. There were also important links between this area and the theatre, though for some this was not so much leisure as a means of making a living.

There were other less common pursuits taking place in the Hungate community, such as linnet singing and aircraft-building.

Linnet Singing

Linnet singing was a favourite pastime in this area in the late 19th and early 20th century. The York Gazette and Herald printed many articles relating to the York Linnet Singing Society and its competitions. Contests were often held at the Black Swan or the Woolpack, both on Peasholme Green. Occasionally meetings also took place at the Slip Inn on Carmelite Street (Easter 1880), the Bricklayer's Arms, Palmer Lane (from 1880 until 1915), the Wheatsheaf and the Haymarket Inn in 1887.

Reg Deighton's father was a competition judge and he remembers vividly these occasions,

They used to have it in the Wheatsheaf pub. And each man used to have his own linnet, a cock linnet of course; they used to bring 'em into the pub and put a board between the two linnets. My dad used to whistle to start 'em off.

Wheatsheaf Inn and Forage Warehouse, 1920s

The birds used to start answering each other over the board - because they couldn't see. My dad used to judge which was the best bird, which had the longest sort of vocabulary of whistling, because he could whistle like a linnet. This used to happen about every other month, and specially round spring time when the birds used to whistle best and he used to come home drunk. There used to be a row every Sunday he came home drunk, so in our house me mother used to hate linnet whistling. It used to be a common thing for people to have a canary, or a linnet; a wild linnet, they used to catch them themselves.

Where they used to catch them mostly was down St Nicholas Park, at the back of Layerthorpe - towards Rawdon Avenue. There used to be something the linnets liked on there - and of course the lads'd go and catch 'em with birdlime and nets. It was legal in those days to do it, but you can't do it now.

And they used to have little boxes, put 'em outside and linnets used to whistle to each other. Johnny Smith would have a good bird, so his neighbour would hang his bird near it, so that when it started whistling the younger bird would learn it all. They used to poach the whistlings of each others' birds. So when it was time to start the competition, they used to keep the birds in so the others didn't learn off them. There were stories of Cockneys that used to fetch bullfinches up from London, but they used to burn their eyes out to make 'em whistle more. I've never actually witnessed that. But everybody had linnets or a canary. Used to be fantastic.

The Yorkshire Evening Press described a visit to a contest in April 1908, stressing the fact that singing was not the same thing as twittering. The judges had to be able to recognise the difference.

A bird might spend ten minutes chattering incessantly without gaining a single point. His opponent might sing a dozen notes and score several points. They are judged solely on the quality of the notes they produce, and the number of changes in their song. The judge can unerringly pick out the good from the bad notes, and can recognise without the least difficulty every slight change in the trills. When two birds get fairly started in their rivalry of song, the judge must be smart indeed to note all the subtle changes, most of them quite imperceptible to the layman. Among the changes are 'cobbler's reeling', 'scraping', 'bubbling' and 'whinneying', all of which have their separate values in points. These the judge marks down on a sheet of paper as the birds are calling against each other.

The birds (all male) were brought into the room in twos, and initially hidden behind panels. When these were removed, they were allowed to see each other for one minute, then given nine minutes to show what they could do. The judges let them see each other and then they would try to outdo their opponents, in a kind of macho display of singing.

Sport

Rugby was popular in the locality, and Mr Wally Holmes was a keen player,

One of the highlights of Hungate was the Woolpack Inn at the side of Peasholme Green, the landlady being Maud Walker and the rugby team which came from there was renowned round York area.

The Leeds Arms entered the interworks once or twice. But the lads drifted back to the Woolpack. That's the sort of character Maud Walker was, a lovable person.

Woolpack Inn and St Saviour's Place, 1930s

The Yorkshire Evening Press of January 1933 reported a glorious win by Woolpack Rovers over South Bank team on the Knavesmire. The Rovers won 19-3 and Deighton converted the final two tries.

Mr Chittock also spoke highly of the place,

There was a landlady, Mrs Walker they called her, just like her on Coronation Street. But she was a gem of a woman, her husband died and she was landlady right up to the Second World War. Even in those days, you came home on leave and you went down the Woolpack for a drink 'cos that's where you always started from. And they run the local interworks rugby teams from the Woolpack. That was a famous thing because they used to carry off the interworks trophy, year after year.

Woolpack Inn, now Minet Insurance, and Blue Coat School, 1995

A rather less common sport was dog racing, described by Reg Deighton,

You used to have whippet racing on Bad Bargain Lane. Used to go rag racing, with whippets and cross-whippet/greyhounds. They used to just have an old iron mangle, used to wind it and they used to have all the cogs so they'd pull a rabbit skin along the road. The dogs used to chase 'em but the original rag-racing was where somebody used to hold a rag and shout, hence its name rag-racing. And they used to race about a hundred and fifty yards, straight, and the dog used to jump up into the winners' arms. Of course it was his dog. That's how they used to finish, by the dogs running up to their owners and getting their reward like a piece of raw meat.

Andy Waudby's cousin kept whippets and they took them to race at Bad Bargain Lane,

One man would hold its neck, and the other man shook a rag in front shouting, 'hi lass'. Each dog had a number on a woollen collar. I would wave the rag for the dogs and got paid two and sixpence.

Sometimes boys could earn a bit of money if they were willing to amuse adults, as Andy found out,

Grown-up men got the lads to box each other with bare knuckles for sixpence, or you could get threepence to get on a box and sing.

The Flying Flea

One member of the Waudby family was a mechanic, and he had a workshop in a street off Hungate, where he built an aeroplane called the Flying Flea. Reg Deighton describes it:

It had a Norton motorbike engine and he used to take the wing off, and took it up to the Knavesmire and tried to fly it and it crashed. And there was a lot after that, a lot of local motor engineers in York started building them, and the one I remember was a feller whose son run York Taxis. He built one of them and then he walked into the blade of it and he had all his shoulder smashed.

I never saw them fly. I read in the morning paper that one had flown in Birmingham. They had proper fuselages, and the cockpit used to come to about four foot off the ground and they used to climb in. They just had one wing, or

maybe two wings, but they was just lads who was experimenting. Engineers who could fit an engine to it and make a propeller go round. Then used to put a body on to it. That's all they were really.

One of Waudby's lads built it and took it up on Knavesmire, and it didn't fly. It was painted red. Great thing to see, it all being pulled down, and he took its wings and body separate down and attached 'em on Knavesmire.

Cinema

In the 1920s and 30s York had many cinemas. The nearest to the Hungate area was the Electric in Fossgate, which is now Macdonalds Furniture Showroom. It had first opened in 1911, and remained open until 1957 (briefly being called the Scala from 1951 until it closed). Mrs Aldrich was a frequent visitor,

They used to call it the Flea Bin, the Flea House. It cost threepence on Saturday afternoon. Used to go and watch Tom Mix, cowboy, in instalments there, and my brother used to go Friday nights and I used to go Saturday night and I would ask him what the serial ended like. It always used to be where he was going to his death, but when you got back next week they'd sort of moved it back a bit somehow and he didn't go over the cliff. There used to be a piano playing music as they was going on their horses, or a violin where the sob stuff come on. Where the girl was getting attacked by the man.

For Mr Holmes, Saturday afternoon was a time to look forward to,

We used to go round to the Electric Cinema in Fossgate. Now admission there was a jam jar, a nice clean jam jar. We'd go in there, watch the films, enjoy ourselves and when coming out started it was all snap crackle and pop, walking over peanut shells.

The jam jars would then be taken to Clancy's, according to Mrs Butterworth,

At the Picture Theatre in Fossgate, they used to take jam jars and things like that in payment - they'd go and cash them in at Clancy's. We'd take our jam jars back to the shop, ha'penny for a small one, and penny for a big one. That's what we used to do ... We've taken rags to Clancy's for coppers.

Andy Waudby was also a regular,

We called the Electric Theatre - 'laugh and scratch'. Many a night on a Friday or Saturday, we've gone and stood in Fossgate in front of Electric Theatre, in the full queue for the fourpennies. We'd go to Sally Dixon's in Garden Place, there, get a ha'porth of carrots, sell these carrots. And we used to queue there and Big Stan'd say, ' Get off t'flags - ear'ole - get over there. I'll tell my cousin of you - he'll thump yer'.

Stan was the commissionaire. He was a bighead, allus pushing us about. And he had to keep us in the gutter, away from the flags. Anyhow, we'd get in the picture, eat our carrots, never say a word to anybody. Sometimes one lad would pay to go in and after five minutes he would go to the toilet and open the window to let all the other lads in.

Then some nights, we'd say, 'we're going to the stalls (Parliament Street Market)', under the stalls, start at one end, 'cos you had a long line of front stalls, right past Marks and Spencers. We used to stand up underneath and get damaged tomatoes, damaged buns, damaged oranges and apples. But the stallholders never used to say nowt to us. Some of 'em used to give us just a bit. A lot had sympathy for us. And it was wonderful. Really wonderful.

Mrs Kay remembers the treats which were an added extra,

So what we used to do when we went to the pictures when we was kids - was what was called the threepenny rush. Saturday afternoon. If you were lucky and your mums could afford it, you got threepence. Or if you couldn't get threepence, they'd let you in for a penny ha'penny. But you had to sit on the front row for that. And that was a really good treat was a Saturday afternoon. Sometimes when you got there they'd give you an apple, to go in with...not every time but just odd occasions. I remember the organ - they was silent

The Electric Theatre, now Macdonalds, Fossgate, 1995

movies as well as talkies, it was always a two part programme. And it got packed, they used to come from all over York, and everybody had a good time.

Christmas time we got a treat from them... a bag when you went in, with an apple, an orange and a pear. But if you were caught making a noise you were thrown out. You had to behave, and quite often there was quite a lot of them thrown out by the scruff of the neck. But we were always good little children!

Mr Thompson enjoyed music hall at the Empire,

Florrie Ford came there. We could go for fourpence in the gods, right at the top and that used to be our Saturday night out. Get a packet of peanuts and throw 'em over the top at the people down below. Or we used to go down Coney Street, they called it the monkey run.

Andy Waudby also remembers the Victoria Hall in Goodramgate, one of York's first cinemas, which opened in 1908. It closed in 1930.

And the Victoria Palace, Palley, got on fire at one time. That was a bit earlier, well when I was a young lad, it was closing then.

Mrs Greenley went there on Saturdays,

All the entertainment was Victoria Hall ... in St Andrewgate. Penny in the bucket. We were lucky if we went, Grandma used to give us a penny. Silent pictures. I remember who was on, Pearl White.

The rear entrance was actually in Aldwark, and Mrs Aldrich knew of it when it was briefly called the Scala (1928 to 1930),

There was a picture house in Aldwark, the Scala, but I don't think a lot remember that one.

Reg Deighton could see the cinema from his house,

My sisters and I used to have to go to bed early and on a Saturday night we used to look straight across from our bedroom into the Albany Hall windows and watch 'em dancing, and of course we used to do that until we fell asleep. Next to the Albany Hall was the back of the Scala Cinema. It was empty at the time, but it was still a cinema. The entrance was in Goodramgate but all the exits, the fire exits, came out at the back.

In later years, some people ventured further afield. Mrs Valerie Law went to the Regal in Piccadilly (which became the ABC in 1961, and is now Marks and Spencers) with her sister, although it occasionally got flooded.

The lady there used to say to my Mum, 'Are you sure she's not 12?', because I was tall. 'No, she's not 12.' And when I was 12 (the age for full price) I took her my birthday cards to show her. We went to ABC Minors on Saturday morning. It was the children's show and if it was your birthday you went up on the stage and they sang happy birthday and you might get a present.

Most people couldn't afford to pay for their entertainment, and when they started courting, the most common practice was to go for walks. This was not without its hazards, as Mrs Hall recalls,

One night we walked all round Heslington and it was freezing and we stood canoodling in a lane. Once we got lost up Tang Hall Lane - a fog came down.

And Mr Hall, "climbed up a lamp-post to see where we were."

Before couples actually started going out together, they would often meet whilst out walking, and this is what Mrs Hall did,

After church my friend and I would go walking down Coney Street. That's what you did when you were in your teens, looking for boyfriends, up and down, up and down, and then down by the river. I used to love to go to that church.

Mr and Mrs Hall, 1995

St Saviour's parish in 1900 certainly had a profusion of public houses, and there were dozens more down nearby Fossgate and Walmgate. By 1920, the Square and Compass in Wesley Place, the Duke's Head in Aldwark, the Whale Fishery on the corner of Haver Lane (so-called because the landlord had been a harpooner in the polar seas) and the Old Sand Hill in St Andrewgate had all disappeared. But a number of inns remained. Aldwark still had the Rose and Crown, Palmer Lane boasted the Bricklayer's Arms, the Garden Gate stood at the top of Carmelite Street and there were three on Peasholme Green - the Black Swan, the Woolpack, and the Leeds Arms. The Turk's Head was still in St Andrewgate (replaced today by Turk's Head Court), and the George Hotel on the corner of Whip-ma-whop-ma-gate (now the Halifax Building Society). The Wheatsheaf was situated in Hungate itself.

Mrs Sheard was actually born and brought up in two pubs,

I was born in the Black Swan, 1911. We stayed there for about four years and then we moved across the road to the Woolpack Inn, where quite a lot of the customers from the Black Swan followed my dad. It was sort of one big happy family. They were such friendly people. When the men were leaving work from Leetham's Mill in Hungate, the clatter of the clogs across Haymarket was really noisy. And there was one man, especially at payday, he would come straight to the pub for his beer. My father was very understanding, and he knew that he had a large family, and he couldn't afford to be drinking, so he always used to say to him - 'I'll let you have one pint now, go home, take your money to your wife, then come back if she gives you any change'.

Mrs Rene Sheard, 1995

There was a tiny little bar, it only seated about four people, and then there was this shelf, the counter with the till underneath it - one of the old fashioned tills you pulled down. I can always remember there was coppers and small silver on the shelf near the glasses. One day he caught a chap with a stick - with a bit of chewing gum, sticky stuff, dabbing to get the money.

We had the old-fashioned pumps for the beer, with a tray and the old mugs underneath. As soon as I realised, I were drinking out the mugs. Mother didn't know where to find me. I was fast asleep, couldn't wake me up - I was kalied.

The inside of the pub was very comfortable. There was a little passage you entered, and the men's dominoes, on the left-hand side, and then there was the bar in the middle and a little private room, the best room; and behind that was a massive ballroom, a great big long room, like a concert room with a stage at the end.

There was a yard where the beer used to be delivered, and of course I was always up there, always noseying. There was this long passage from the bar up to the cellar. Me mam used to have a lady helping her, she used to do the washing up there. And dad used to keep his hundred proof spirits in the big stone jars behind a curtain in the living-kitchen, which looked right onto Haymarket. Now many times she'd be fast asleep in a chair - she'd been helping herself to the proofed stuff.

The policemen always came in twos to the pub. Always made theirselves at home in t'kitchen with pints. I was pulling ale at nine or ten. I liked to be in it.

Mrs Fearn remembers,

There was a pub at the top of Dundas Street, and the landlady that had it was daughter to Mr and Mrs Barker. Midwife and undertaker.

I know it was a pub because they had a big grate that went down into cellars. Used to lift it up when draymen used to come to put fresh barrels in. And I looked down there one day and saw a ten shilling note. And I said to my father, 'I've just seen a ten shilling note...I can't reach it'. We got a big piece of string and a safety pin and he stayed there for ages and ages and he got that ten shilling note out.

The Garden Gate was in Brunswick Street, Brass Rapper Row. Just prior to it all being pulled down. And they used to pull our Magnet beer down in cellar. And our entertainment on a Saturday night, when you was older, was, there was these seven or eight pubs, and you'd probably go off somewhere, to the pictures or to the Empire.

Some people might use the pub as an off-licence, like Mrs Hall's family,

Me grandad liked a drink and grandma used to go to the Garden Gate for him. She used to bring him a pint in a jug if he didn't want to go out.

And Mrs Thompson's family too,

On a Friday night all t'relations came. They used to come about four o'clock, they used to be there till maybe midnight. And then they used to go with the jug down to the pub, and get a jug full of beer, and then they'd be all singing and dancing at the end o't lane.

Her sister Mrs Felton also remembers these occasions,

My Granny...would make these big meat pies and a big pan of mushy peas, and they used to have pie and peas on a Friday. Real good old days them.

Of course, drink was a real problem for many people and caused misery for a lot of families. Many people drank to forget their problems though the enjoyment was only short-lived. Yet drinking was a priority with many men and women, as George Squire recalls,

They say soap and water was cheap but all the money went in booze. The pubs were bouncing with people on a Friday, Saturday night. I used to stand outside. They never had money for food but they always had money for booze, dinner time and night. I used to sit on the wall at the Garden Gate and women used to dance on the tables.

Mr Jack Birch knew of an alternative,

At that time, gin was relatively cheap, and there were many gin houses, particularly in the Walmgate area. Now the original company called the York Coffee House Company, was created to provide an alternative drink and they provided a coffee house in Walmgate, with warmed rooms, so that men particularly, could go and be warm and drink coffee instead of gin. It became, in fact, quite a successful undertaking and moved from Walmgate and entered into the catering business in the city.

One of the public houses also doubled up as a soup-kitchen, to alleviate some of the poverty which was being experienced. Mr Ted Chittock remembers,

Now the Bricklayer's Arms was a pub during the night but it served as a soup kitchen during the day. That was the main meal of the day for lots of people, because they were out of work and they used to go there for probably a penny or tuppence for a bowl of soup and that fed the family. A very prominent lady ran that. Call her Miss Ramsay. She was head of the RSPCA.

Theatre

The theatre was not really a working-class pastime, but as well as the rather more middle-class Theatre Royal, York also offered entertainment in the shape of the Empire, which often presented music-hall. Many of the artistes appearing at the Empire lodged in the St Saviourgate/Spen Lane area, and caused much interest amongst the residents.

Mr James Cave lived at 'Rock House', St Saviourgate, opposite St Saviour's Church. He remembers watching from his front room window on a Sunday afternoon and seeing these entertainers arrive. Mrs Reynolds even saw Jessie Matthews and Gracie Fields walking down St Saviourgate.

When actors were appearing for any length of time, they would put their children into the local school. Rene Wright (Mrs Sheard) met a lot of them at her school, and remembers,

the hours I've spent at the back of the stage at York Empire with these children and their families - because I was always interested in all this dancing business and dressing up.

Mrs Greenley's mother in Spen Lane took lodgers in on Sundays, including one leading lady from the Blue Hens,

She was a right drinker and she was on at night, and she'd been out all afternoon and she came in and she was well overboard. Me mam and me looked after her and got her sobered up and got her coffee to go to the theatre at night. I remember that 'cos she was well away.

Mrs May Greenley, 1995

May Fearn, 1928

There were also Russians staying there. They left a walking stick at the back of the door so that it would fall on anyone who came into their room. No animals were allowed but one Sunday a couple arrived carrying a basket. Mrs Greenley remembers,

Me mam says to me 'go upstairs and take them a cup of tea' and when I got up there, there was two monkeys on the bed. So she told them to get out.

As May Fearn, Mrs Greenley herself loved the theatre. When she was seventeen, she accompanied a friend who wanted to audition for 'Mother Goose' but instead of the friend, she herself was chosen to be in the chorus, and had to dress as a chicken, and then wear a riding habit.

I could go for the first house but not for the second. My uncle had to come and collect me at 7.30. I liked it and I wanted to keep going but my mam said no, it wasn't right. I got seventeen shillings that week.

St Saviourgate had its own actor, Reginald Beckwith, who also wrote plays. He began his career as an amateur with the Everyman Theatre in York Guildhall, then joined Henry Baynton's Shakespearian Company. Several of his plays were broadcast on radio and TV and he went on to appear in many films, mostly light comedies including 'Genevieve', 'The Runaway Bus', 'The Captain's Table' and the thriller 'The Thirty-Nine Steps', before his career was cut short by his death at Bourne End, Bucks., in 1965 at the age of 56.

Another means of entertainment was music, as Mr Cave knew,

I've been a musician all my life, as a semi-professional. Used to get half a crown an hour. I started at seven years of age with the violin. Carried on for several years and then broke into sport and neglected that. Picked it up again. In the '30s we won the All Yorkshire Dance Competition in 1932. Louis Armstrong appeared on the same night at the Rialto. We were resident band at Royal Station Hotel for years. Played two nights a week, sometimes three or four, you take it when it comes. Dance bands - the whole of York was keen.

I played clarinet, alto saxophone and violin. I used to sight read, was a big advantage. I played with Bert Keech at the De Grey Rooms, the Modernaires, the Rialtonians, occasionally. If anybody got let down, there were two or three of us could fill in, in any position.

A lot of voluntary places including Naburn, Clifton, Bootham, Deighton Grove hospitals. We played and they sketched. Someone supplied tea and biscuits. We enjoyed it as much. You were free and easy. De Grey Rooms, Assembly Rooms, Albany Hall in Goodramgate, Ebor Hall, Davy Hall, Grand ballroom, Rialto. A lot of dancing took place in those years. There were 40 dance bands on one week. Our biggest band was a ten piece, mainly six. Couldn't afford to pay too many. I had a motorbike, about 18 to 20. AJS and Norton were absolutely great. I used to go all over. You could leave your motorbike outside the house all night and nobody would touch it. XL petrol was tenpence halfpenny a gallon.

Rear of 1-17 Lower Wesley Place, 1930s

7

Poverty and the Community Spirit

Health and the Medical Profession

In the 1920s and '30s disease was rife, and medical treatment had to be paid for. A lot of people could not afford a doctor as Andy Waudby recalls,

Disease was right round 'em. And it were there and these doctors were fighting the disease. You've got the slaughterhouses. You got the ingredients for all the diseases under the sun. But this is life in Hungate. You'll get the old women stood at doorstep and they're all what we call 'calling' (with a flat 'a'). They'll stand there, they've got a flat cap on, they've got arms like ham shanks. Immediately a woman went sick, the woman next door fed the kids and the man. It was fantastic. Oh ay, they'd muck in and help you. There was a lot of this home medicine stuff. Ginger, lemon or summat. Dash down to see Mrs Bardy to see if she's got some ginger.

As soon as a woman went sick, the minute the woman next door would find out about it, that woman came in to see to her before they ever thought of doctors. Because, don't forget, you're having to pay doctors. They had what you call a club - tuppence a week.

I take me hat off to these doctors because they allowed you to pay tuppence or threepence a week. How the doctors lived - well it beats me because they had to rely on tuppences and threepences - to get their money.

Mr Thompson remembers,

There was a lot of illness. Consumption, or TB, but you didn't get these strokes like now. People didn't live so long, they died younger. When you got TB, it's a chesty thing. They used to send 'em to the sanatorium - at Fairfields. They used to put you in there and you used to have to sleep with the windows open. Fresh air was supposed to be the cure. If you was in hospital, somebody'd do your washing and somebody'd feed the kiddies.

There were a couple living at the top of Hungate, William and Ellen Barker, who were the resident midwife and undertaker. As Wally Holmes observes,

Mr and Mrs Barker. She brought 'em into the world, he took 'em out again.

Mrs Sheard remembers Mrs Barker the midwife,

Mrs Barker was a wonderful lady. And she'd a long black coat and midwife bag. I lived in, my first little house, in Layerthorpe - Radnor Street, and I used to go down to mam's every day - just over the bridge to Haymarket. I'd go down and when I was getting pretty well away with me pregnancy, mam says, 'Rene, you didn't half pull a face when you were going up'. 'Oh, just a twinge or two, I have mam.' She says, 'Go down to Granny Barker's and tell her'. Granny Barker says, 'Get your dad to take you straight home, and don't come out of the place any more'. And she told me what to do with my bed - to get organised. She said I could have had it in the street, that bairn. Anyway, it were ten pound born. But I went upstairs, and I hadn't been upstairs a couple of minutes and that child was started to be born. Actually, before I got on the bed, and if I hadn't gone to Granny Barker's I wouldn't have had me bed all prepared. And she said, 'Plenty o' newspapers and brown paper, lass'.

When Mrs Barker was called to a person in labour, the beds had to be covered with sheets to prevent the children from seeing what was going on - at the birth of the new baby.

Mrs Cook was the granddaughter of the Barkers,

Grandad had funerals. Grandma was midwife, she got thirty shillings for delivering the baby and tending for ten days. Grandma used to wear a black alpaca skirt and linen skirt underneath and a flannelette skirt which she'd take off to wrap baby in.

Then there were the school clinics, as Mrs Fearn describes,

Of course, you got to school and there was the school clinics. We used to go there for everything - eyes, teeth, tonsils, everything. Manicure, you name it. They'd have taken Uncle Billy's job and cut your hair as well. In fact they used to do if you used to go with dirty hair - they used to take the lot of that off.

They used to paint your tonsils. Used to have a big long brush and they used to put this yellow stuff on, and it used to tickle, just imagine anyone tickling your tonsils with a brush. I mean kids used to be sick and then he'd bundle you out and he was really mad, he used to get really cross with you. And if they did your teeth, you went to dentist part to have your teeth done, used to give you an injection into your gums. I mean now when you go to dentist he waits, doesn't he, and he sort of rubs your gums around and waits. It was the needle - you was holding on to his hand, like this while he was taking your teeth out. We had it rough.

Mr Holmes sometimes had to go to the 'unction clinic',

I used to go as a bairn to Castlegate, and when I come to go over Foss Bridge, y'can tell how big I was. I used to put me head through, watch the ducks and everything there, and come back and go over Piccadilly Bridge and down the steps into Castlegate School. Also in Piccadilly there, there was the blue unction. Wooden Hut. We used to go there. Now that was the school clinic. Used to go for your unction and they dabbed blue unction on all your sores and everything.

Samuel Thompson during World War II

Samuel Thompson recalls,

If you were sick you had to go to the dispensary and you had to get a dispensary note for the doctor to come and see you. It cost you two shillings for a visit. Dispensary note had to be signed by a vicar, or a policeman, and you used to go to Duncombe Place to the dispensary. You had to go and sit inside in the queue and they'd give you a bottle of black medicine, and the most popular thing was brimstone and treacle!

School clinic used to be in Piccadilly, go there for everything, toothache and headache. They used to get a pair of pliers and pop some cotton wool and dip it in iodine, put it in your mouth and paint your tonsils with it. Everybody got that. Every time you got laryngitis. You used to have a nurse come round and look at your hair for nits.

Samuel Thompson, 1995

The local doctors themselves seemed to be interesting characters and there were three who are remembered with affection. Dr Walter Kelly, Dr Reynolds and Dr Dench, father of the actress Dame Judi Dench.

According to Mrs Kay, Dr Kelly was,

a character. And he swore like a trooper. I never really met Dr Kelly until I was about seventeen but I'd heard an awful lot about him. He was good with the people, he was a down to earth man. In those days you didn't make appointments - you just sat. Anyway all of a sudden the door opened to one of these rooms and this voice said, 'Well if none of you buggers wants to see me I might as well bloody go home'. But this was his manner. I thought he was absolutely great. I never saw another doctor after that but him.

And we were panel patients. Mum paid threepence a week...and it paid for all your medicine. And it paid for you to go into hospital as well. We used to take our threepence into Pavement - there was an upstairs office. We never went to a dispensary. Because we paid into this scheme.

There was a big flu epidemic. It was before my time. And my granny, she had just had a little boy. There was four sisters and this boy. I think he was a few month old and then they had a big flu epidemic, so my mum lost her mother, her brother and two sisters all in one week. My mother worked at the laundry at the end of Dodsworth Avenue, the Ideal Laundry. She was seventeen. So when they died, my grandad said, 'Right, you have to look after us'.

Jack Birch remembers the flu epidemic,

St Saviour's Church at that time was in full use and I remember being in bed in the attic hearing the bells toll for the departed. I convinced myself that I was probably another one of those in a short time, but that never, fortunately, happened. Funeral services were a very elaborate affair, with the carriages drawn by horses, decked out with black plumes, and black trimmings to the carriage. Really quite impressive.

Mrs Reynolds recalls one evening when,

Dr Kelly ... was going down, he'd forgot the number but there were several lights on and it was midnight and so very dark, and eventually, he called out, 'Who the hell wants Kelly?'

Mrs Fearn also knew Dr Kelly,

Dr Kelly's vocabulary was noted. I used to work at Ideal Laundry, and these people that lived in this house, when I used to cut up Fetter Lane, we really got to know them. Used to pop in on my way to work to say hello. The old chap there, he was very, very bad with his chest, and he was an elderly man then when I was, what, sixteen, seventeen, going to work. Dr Kelly was his doctor. I remember him telling us one day that he'd been to see him and he'd leave him this special medicine. He was complaining it hadn't done him any good and he'd been coming over Ouse Bridge and met this friend of his. He was puffing and blowing, so they talked and the friend said to him, 'You don't want to be taking any of these medicines. You want to use Vick. Don't rub it in, get it by half-spoonful and put it on the back of your tongue and swaller it'. So he did. And when Dr Kelly went to see him, he said, 'Well there's a big improvement here, it must be paying off, this medicine I'm giving you'. But he said, 'I haven't taken any of your bloody medicine'. And he told him he'd been taking this Vick, so Dr Kelly said, 'Well go and get another bloody jar and take that because it's done you more good than this medicine'. And that's the type of doctor he was.

Mrs Reynolds and her son Guy King-Reynolds were exposed to disease because her husband Dr Reynolds had to work amongst it,

We used to catch most of them. Scarlet fever, my father caught that and was sent to the isolation hospital. We all had that. And TB. And evacuate. Seal the doors and pump it full of whatever it was, sulphur or something, then we could all move back in. But father had mumps and scarlet fever.

I remember father coming back, he knew a family and he said, 'I've just been and she's got TB', and they called it in those days, galloping consumption. And

I remember a short time afterwards he came back, it must be only days, and he said, 'There's nothing we can do, she's gone'. In no time at all they haemorrhaged and that was it.

In the old days it was the Guardians, not public assistance like it is now. My husband had a TB case down Kendal's Passage and she had been in Fairfields Sanatorium. And she worked at the Hygienic Laundry and of course with working in the laundry and having TB it came back again. And she said, 'Please Doctor, don't let me go back', and all the neighbours said, 'You mustn't let her go back, we'll look after her'. They were wonderful people. Now the Doctor of Health, he was a shocker. He really was horrible and he insisted she go to Fairfield and my husband said, 'No, she's not going. She's going to be well looked after, the neighbours say they'll do this and I'll see that they do'.

'Then in that case we'll stop her voucher.' And they did. And my husband said, 'I'll provide the voucher', and they had quite a fight. And my husband was on the health committee. They had a terrible fight and eventually my husband won. She didn't go and my husband did provide the vouchers, you could not get a thing out of the Guardians in those days.

Everyone seemed to admire the doctor, including Mrs Fearn,

Everybody loved Dr Reynolds, he'd come down there to you, no matter what hour of the day or night it was. It didn't matter if you had two hundred quid in your purse or tuppence, you was his patient. He was a marvellous man. No discriminating against you because you was from Hungate.

Mr King-Reynolds and his mother describe Dr Reynolds,

Father was a local doctor and consequently most of these people in Hungate and Layerthorpe were what was then called his panel patients.

He was also police surgeon and I suppose one or two of them got to know him in other circumstances too - after a very good Saturday night. He did a lot of work with Seebohm Rowntree, who published that famous document on Poverty in York. And he did a lot of work because obviously he was seeing a great deal of real poverty. I can remember food parcels going out, some of the children without shoes.

He was the first Labour councillor for the Guildhall Ward of York, which was quite astonishing. He used to tell a funny story, of him standing as a Labour councillor and some of his patients, bless 'em, were as poor as church mice, and would come into his surgery and say, 'Doctor, you're not standing for t'council? Standing for council's great but not for Labour doctor, not for Labour.' They expected him to be Conservative but he was what you'd call an old fashioned Labour... he was just appalled by the poverty he was working under, which was absolutely the antithesis of his father, who was a staunch Conservative, and was slightly horrified that his son was standing for the council as a Labour man, for which he was then duly elected as a councillor. In 1929 they won Guildhall Ward for the first time in history. It had been Conservative all the time.

The only time I remember father being attacked was when he was called by the neighbours. In those days doctors were much more, sort of priests as well, social workers. It was one Christmas Day and he was called. A little child came to the door and said, 'Oh, doctor will you come please, separate father and mother', and it was Christmas Day and we were going to sit down to Christmas dinner.

He stopped it and then the wife turned on him, 'you leave him alone!' He was called out three or four times a night, very often to drunks. In the old days, in the police station, was a notice on the wall. They could ask for a bed and ask for a blanket, or ask to see a doctor - and this was on the police wall in those days - and believe me they did get called out. And we had one of those speaking tubes from the street. And he used to make 'em walk a straight line and say things like 'Burgess's fish sauce shop'.

And of course he used to be called out as police surgeon when they fished bodies out of the river. I remember my father coming back, somebody had been in the river for about six months and the policeman said, 'You'd better hold your nose doctor, it's a bit meller'.

YORK MUNICIPAL ELECTION

FRIDAY, 1st NOVEMBER, 1929
POLLING 8-0 a.m. to 8-0 p.m.

The GUILDHALL Ward

LABOUR CANDIDATE

H. E. KING REYNOLDS
SOLICITS
YOUR VOTE AND INTEREST

Printed by Wood & Richardson Limited, 2, King's Square, York
and Published by James D. A. Law, 2, Railway Street, York

Dr Reynolds' election pamphlet, 1929

I remember father telling us that lovely story of people coming to see him with a bad foot, for instance, and he would examine the foot and he said, 'Take off your other sock,' and there'd be a horrified silence and, 'I haven't washed it'. Yes, they'd washed the one foot and not the other one. Again you've got to realise these are cold taps outside.

There was a lot of rickets though, and bow-legged kids. And with those very high boots with a big heel, what do you call 'em, club-feet. I mean there was medicine but still it was, in terms of rectifying malformations, non-existent. If you were born like that well it was hard luck - you struggled.

And there was the workhouse too, which everyone dreaded. And that was a great shock, when they started talking about taking away the workhouse. You go in and could have a bath and a breakfast, but you had to work, just break wood or something. But there was somewhere to go. Now there isn't.

Poverty and the Community Spirit

The parish was very poor, yet the poverty and deprivation meant that people shared with each other, as they were 'all in the same boat'. The community fostered the spirit of mutual help and care, without much aid from outside. Institutions such as the Church were supportive to an extent, but there were certain individuals who were genuinely concerned, as Mr Waudby testifies,

You had Reverend Pyne doing what he could, Dr Reynolds, Miss Ramsay and you had Mr Pickering. Now he had the bookshop in High Ousegate before the Shambles...he belonged to the Centenary Chapel, that was in St Saviourgate. Now I had occasion to meet some of the people that went to Centenary Chapel, and they were so kind. Mr Pickering was such a wonderful chap...and I remember he used to come on a bike and take us for scouts.

Reverend Pyne of St Cuthbert's... He didn't wait for you to go to church, he brought the church to you. The bishops in their fine palaces and posh cars were

nowhere to be seen when it meant practising Christianity. On a cold night we went to a small meeting house which belonged the Band of Hope. A nice warm hall with forms. Miss Ramsay gave us soup and sweets and we would say prayers and sing hymns. They'd teach us how to love and pray.

So through poverty and this suffering, they had this feeling for others, regardless of what colour you were. Now I went to school with Chinese sons. Now we accept 'em, straight away. 'Cos when you're living in poverty, and hard times, you always have a feeling for your fellow man. This is why Hungate people and Walmgate people, and Layerthorpe, they're a wonderful people. They'll give you anything. Anybody knocked at that door and wanted a cup of tea or something to eat, we'd share it with 'em straight away. This is Hungate people. That makes us so proud. Because we feel for others.

They didn't go to church but they were more God-fearing people lived there than there was in the rest o' York. They believed in Jesus and believed in God. Now this is the amazing part about it, but still you wouldn't get 'em going to church.

For all their roughness - by, they could fight as well, the women, they might be rough and ready, they were tough women, but inside were ticking hearts of gold. You knock at a door, they'll share their bit wi' you. If we had people like that nowadays, what a wonderful world it would be.

Mrs Kay explains,

There was a lot of poverty. And Reverend Pyne used to come round and he used to help, he helped everybody. He was a kind man. He saw that people didn't go hungry. If he thought that anybody was, he'd get other people to keep an eye on, and if the neighbours, say 'Well look, these people are desperate', he would see they were all right. As far as he could.

If he thought you were desperate, he would give you the penny and you could get the old big white jug and off y'went to the soup kitchen on Haymarket. That's where we went, me mum used to give us a penny and we'd take a big white jug, and she sent us off and well you could almost eat it with a knife and fork. It was so full of vegetables. Wouldn't say there was much meat - but there was plenty of vegetables.

I had an aunt just lived across the road. We lived at number 5 and she lived across the road from us in this little street, and when she baked she'd stand at the door like this. 'In here', 'What?' 'Never mind what - get in here', and she'd sit us down to a cup of tea and fresh baked bread. And that's how people were. Everybody shared.

Mrs Sheard also respected Mr Pyne,

He was a wonderful man, Reginald Pyne, a wonderful man. He used to come in the pub when the men were enjoying their pints and chat away to them. He was no high up business because he was a vicar.

And Mr Thompson visited another soup kitchen,

In Dundas Street. We used to go with a jug for two pennorth of soup. They all had big families, six or seven in a family. I was the middle one, there was six kids.

Everyone was willing to help in an emergency, in any practical way that they could as Mr Holmes says,

If you wasn't doing any baking, next door neighbour would do it for you and you'd do her shopping. And you went in each other's houses helping 'em wash.

There was allus one person in't street, if somebody was having a baby, they would be there to see it into the world, or if somebody had died, there'd be somebody there to come into your house and lay 'em out for you.

Mrs Aldrich also remembers,

We had a food kitchen on Walmgate and we went there from school for our dinners. Free dinners. They were lovely as well. We went down a passage and

about halfway down at lefthand side. There was loads went. Beautiful an' all. And there was a soup kitchen in St Saviourgate itself.

There was a place down Lady Peckitt's Yard. We went down there and we got some boots what you lace up, and an odd coat or two, but we didn't get much because there were so many wanted them. Some went in their bare feet. They used to get cardboard, or anything and make soles in their shoes, to hide the holes in the outer soles.

If you were lucky you got some things given, but sometimes you used to go errands for old people and they would give you a penny or something like that and you used to take it home to your mother, a penny was a lot in them days, and pay it towards helping your mother.

Mrs Butterworth had the same experience,

I've gone without shoes and socks meself. Well I did once and I was in me bare feet and these people shouted of me, and I daren't stop and so I just ran home and when I told me mam she said, 'Y'soft cat, they might a' been going to buy you some shoes'.

I mean we were poor but we weren't that poor that me mam couldn't feed us. And we were always clean. But as I say nothing posh. But I think our days were better that they are today somehow. I suppose our parents knew how to contrive better than what they do today.

The food that was available always went first to the head of the house, as Mr Thompson knew well,

My father used to get two boiled eggs for his tea on a Friday payday and we used to take it in turns to get the top of the egg. They would put veg and carrots and all sorts in to make soup and that would last you two days. You got soup and that were it. Good old days.

Mr Squire stresses that the classes did not mix,

There was another pub on Dundas Street, where the first soup kitchen opened. Pea soup. You took a jug or a bowl. If you were poor you were poor, if you were wealthy you were wealthy, and they never mixed. People in the houses in St Saviourgate never mixed with Hungate. No way.

If a person became really destitute then the final port of call was the workhouse, as Mr Waudby reflects,

I remember my granny taking in this poor lass, I can just picture her now. And nobody wanted her. My granny had a heart o'gold. My granny took her in for a time, but I don't know if she finished up in the workhouse. She'll have died. The workhouse people were on Huntington Road.

You could always tell a person who was from the workhouse because he had a grey suit. When he got too old and couldn't work any more, he couldn't sit back and get money...He finished up in the workhouse and he got a grey suit and some of 'em used to stop there the night, but they had to chop sticks, before they got food.

The police took away men in strait-jackets who were broken down through despair. Men committed suicide by cutting their throats. Ex-soldiers with legs off, arms off, came round singing for pennies, or sold matches or bootlaces because they could not get work. These men had fought for their country and were promised by the idiots in Parliament that they would come back to a land fit for heroes to live in. It certainly took a hero to live in it! There were men who were breathless, could hardly walk, their lungs shattered by poisoned gas. The wives queued outside the pawnshop on Monday mornings with bedsheets or anything they could sell. First World War soldiers told me how York local councillors urged men to join up and fight but after the war they sat on parish boards cutting men's dole. They told old soldiers to sell their furniture to get money. If you had a piano, your dole was stopped and you were told to sell it.

When I was poorly, I had to go into the infirmary, it was part of the workhouse. You had no money. I had pneumonia in the workhouse.

Andy Waudby in the army, 1939

Andy Waudby with wooden toy marble rack, 1995

I was in the army. Now your blokes in Burmah - biggest part of the blokes who were fighting were either coalmining or blokes out o't slums. The conditions in the jungle were so bad, and you were fighting a tough enemy, the biggest part of your blokes came out o't slums, all over the country, because they were the lads who could go up against the Japanese and fight. They were nigh on starving in the jungle. I had to go without food, that's why I have no muscles. We walked over swamps, jungles, over mountains. The army weren't bloody daft ... picked lads from the slums.

Mrs Fearn remembers the depression when people were reduced to combing the streets to find food and cigarettes,

Well this corner here, Alf Huckle's shop, they used to congregate round there during that depression. Did the men there. We called 'em men, seventeen, eighteen, nineteen.

They were called balls in those days, the dances, and that's what they were. And there was De Grey Rooms and Assembly Rooms. And lovely places now, but then they were all lit up and everything. They used to arrive there in all their evening clothes. The ladies and the men as well. We used to go just to stand and watch. See what clothes they had on. Especially the women, for the girls. And the men used to go in maybe sections of three and they'd take whichever pitch they wanted there, outside Assembly Rooms or go outside De Grey Rooms. And some of 'em used to go outside Empire Theatre. But this was when these big dances were on. And they used to go just for cigar ends. Butt ends of cigarettes. Stick with a pin or whatever it was. They used to put 'em in this tin. And I've watched 'em stood at the top of that street the following day, and they used to share, they'd share what they had. But just imagine - somebody could've thrown them away, they could be chronically ill or something like that. But that's how bad it was. Used to pick these butts up and share them. Break 'em up and they'd be cigarettes rolled there.

For some people, there were alternative options, though these were not always regarded sympathetically, as Mr Squire points out,

They had no money but they had high morals. If a lass got pregnant she was a whore, the illegitimate child was a bastard. The fellers could do as they liked but a woman was either right or wrong, pure or otherwise. There's one family and the daughter came down Hungate with a fur coat on and I was sat outside the shop. What a beautiful lass. 'Oh yes, she's doing well, she's come from working on Piccadilly.' I said, 'Whereabouts in Piccadilly?' and Mickey said, 'Piccadilly in London. She's on t'game.' I says, 'What game?' I couldn't balance it out.

Mr Holmes explains,

As a community though it was a civilisation killed when they moved it. The people may look on us as poor people. We weren't poor at all. What with character and everything else we were rich people. We was happy .... I'll stand on the roof tops and shout it where I was born and where I was fetched up.

Wally Holmes, 1995

Wally Holmes as a young man

Mr Squire found that,

The people were very caring, you didn't do anything wrong because they didn't allow you to, they'd give you a clatter and put you right. There was a lot of intertwining of people and families. They were all very self-opinionated, all the families did well.

They were very sociable. They used to sit out in chairs in the evening in summertime in the street, either knitting or talking across the street. Old Granny Dodd used to nurse 'em all. It was a self-help community.

Mr Cave agrees,

If anybody died, some woman in the street would lay them out. Everybody rallied round. No-one dreamed of opening the curtains, always drew them when a funeral passed. On Sunday at St Saviour's Church, loaves of bread were given out to poor parishioners. People gathered together without having to be asked, the feeling was marvellous.

Mrs Greenley speaks of the same spirit of kindness in her mother,

A girl once came who'd been to St Andrewgate and had a baby in a field. No-one would take her in. Mam was good with people and took her in and she put her a bed on the floor. Next morning she'd gone and taken the blankets. Mother said 'don't call t'police, she must have wanted them'.

And Mrs Fearn sums up the attitude of the Hungate community,

It was marvellous. Everybody helped everybody else. If your mother didn't appear for a full day, your neighbours would pull you up in the street and say 'Where's your mother?' And if you said, 'She isn't very well', they'd come in and they'd bring bread cakes. You never used to lock any doors, at all. Anybody had been in your house when you got back, you knew that they'd been in because there'd be a fruit pie on the table - it was to put something in, not to take something out.

If you lived in that area, I don't care where you went, anywhere in the world, I can honestly say, we looked after one another. You was never allowed to wander. But I mean if you was, everybody knew who you were. If you was out there when you was about eight or nine...they used to take you home. Things like what happen today could never have happened in those days, because you were watched over by every family. It was poor, absolute abject poverty; not saying it wasn't, but by God it was clean.

It was a tough environment, but it wasn't a vicious environment compared to today's standard. These women were this type - if you saw them stood at the street end talking, and obviously they always did, arms folded, sort of having a real good chinwag, and if there was anything matter with you at all, whether you'd fallen, cut yourself, or whether you was wet, miserable, for something that had gone on at home or something like that, you had open arms. You could go to 'em, like everybody was either your mother or your grandmother. You always felt safe. Always.

Everybody's house seemed to be open to everybody else. My mam died when she was early forties. And there was six of us left. And youngest was six months old, and me dad brought us all up. And by God, he got a lot of help. They couldn't do enough for you. I mean, anywhere he had to go for anything, the kids were looked after, and they didn't only take you and look after you, they did for you what you've got to pay baby sitters to do now. They washed you and put you to bed, they had the run of the house and you had the run of their house in return. And there was the depression during this period that I'm talking about as well.

You had to share what you had down Hungate. It was a community and it would be a damn sight better today if there was a few more like it.

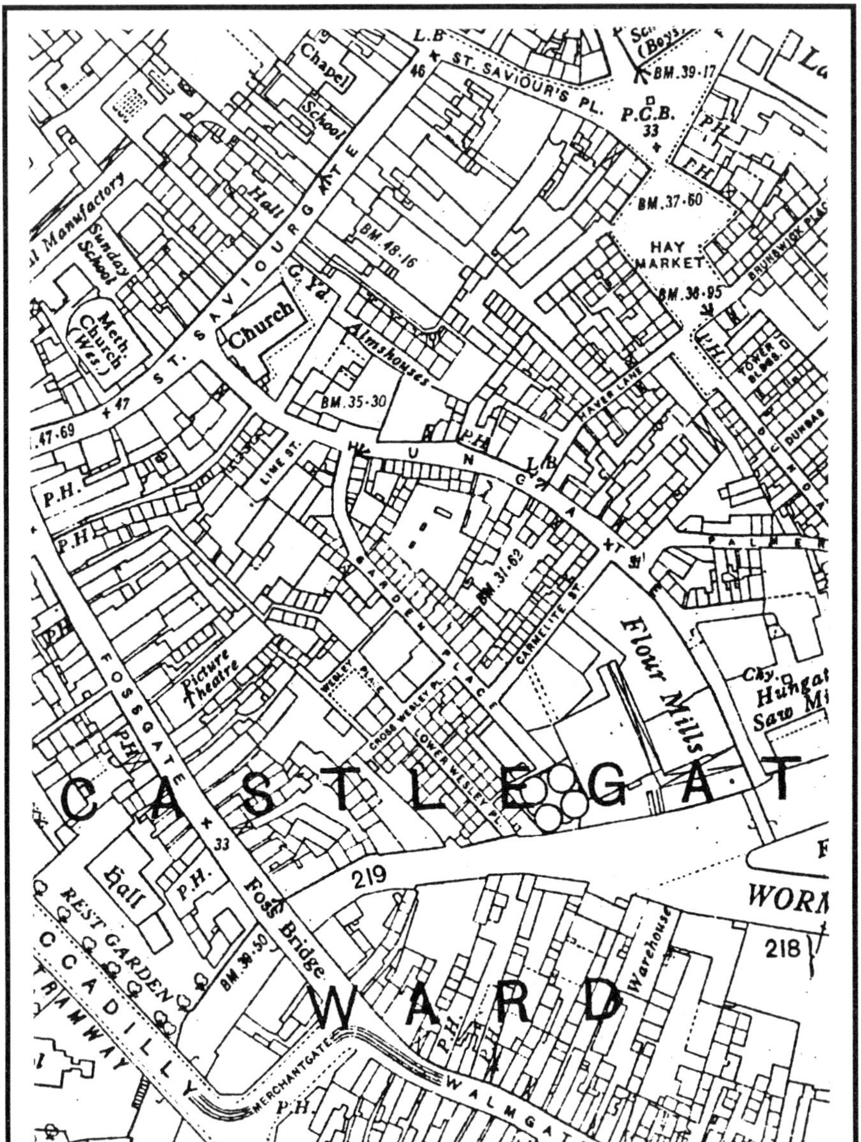

Hungate area, 1930

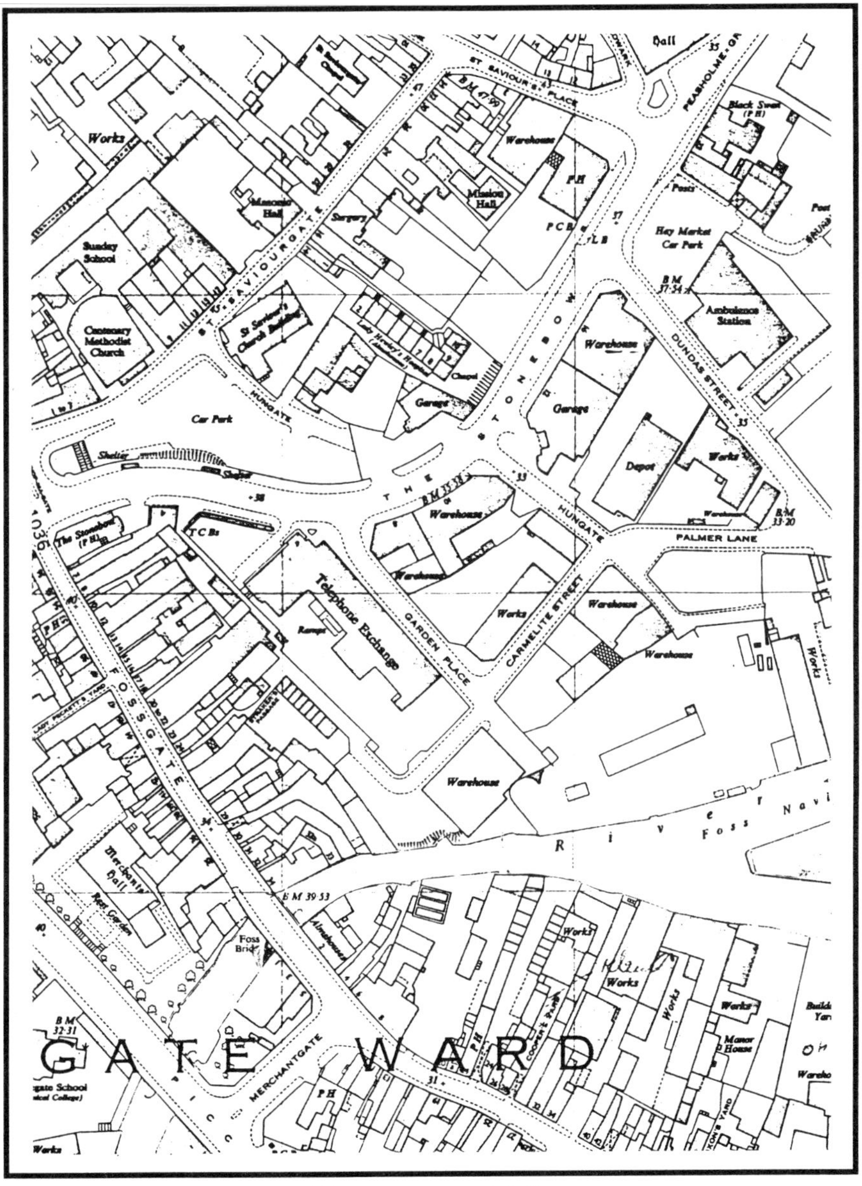

Hungate area, 1961

About the author ...

Van Wilson is a graduate in English and American Studies who has been involved with oral and local history for several years, and has had articles published in several magazines.

She is the author of 'The History of a Community : Fulford Road District' (1984) and 'Alexina : A Woman in Wartime York' (1995).

Van also works as administrator for a youth theatre, and is married with two children.

About the photographer ...

Simon I Hill gained Diplomas in Photography and Art & Design from Blackpool College of Art in 1985, an MA in Independent Film and Television from the London Institute in 1992, and is currently writing his doctoral thesis in an area of Arts Policy and Management with the City University Business School, London. He was elected a Fellow of the Royal Society of Arts in 1989, and of the Royal Photographic Society in 1991. Also in 1991, Simon was selected by Kodak for inclusion in their publication celebrating the best of British photography.

Simon has had photographs published in many national and international journals and periodicles including *The Sunday Times Magazine, National Geographic Magazine, The Illustrated London News,* and *Der Spiegel.*

Formerly Head of Photography with the York Archaeological Trust - an organisation with which he continues to be associated - he is currently Proprietor and Creative Director of Scirebröc - a design group which he founded in 1983. Simon is married with two children.

About the ARC ...

The ARC - Archaeological Resource Centre - is an award-winning hands-on exploration of archaeology for visitors of all ages, designed by the York Archaeological Trust to complement its Jorvik Viking Centre in Coppergate. Located in the beautifully restored medieval church of St Saviour, close to the Shambles, the ARC has an ever-changing programme of special exhibitions, children's activity mornings, lectures, videos and other events throughout the year.

A visit to the ARC begins with a short and informative introductory video narrated by John Craven. Visitors then go on to meet real archaeologists, handle historic finds, learn ancient skills and crafts, and have fun with some of the latest developments with interactive computing. For further information, telephone 01 904 654 324.

The ARC is open all year, including weekends and evenings for pre-booked parties of more than 10 persons. To make a party booking for the ARC or the Jorvik Viking Centre, telephone 01 904 613 711.

Open to the public:	Monday to Friday	10am to 5pm
	Saturday and Sunday	1pm to 5pm

Closed Good Friday and 18-31 December.
Last admission 4.30pm
Special opening arrangements can be made for pre-booked groups.

The ARC is a project of the York Archaeological Trust.
The Trust is a registered charity. Number 509060.

Archaeological Resource Centre
ARC

Bibliography

Harris, A. "Chicory in Yorkshire". Yorkshire Archaeological Journal Vol. 59. 1987

Kelly's and White's Street Directories of York 1898-1950

Knight, C.B. A History of the City of York. Herald Printers. 1944

Watson, A.G. (Ed.) York City Year Book and Business Directory 1909 to 1930. Yorkshire Gazette Newspapers

York City Council Maps of Hungate

York City Council Minutes 1935

York City Council Video. Hungate - a Vanished Community

York City Reference Library. Newspaper Index

York Times. Vol. 3. No. 1. Early Spring 1963

Yorkshire Evening Press. 1908 and 1933